Tarzan and Jane

Tarzan and Jane

How to thrive in the new corporate jungle

Margot Katz

P

PROFILE BOOKS

First published in Great Britain in 2007 by
Profile Books Ltd
3a Exmouth House
Pine Street
Exmouth Market
London EC1R 0JH
www.profilebooks.co.uk

A CIP catalogue record for this book is available from the British Library.

ISBN 978 1 84668 002 1

Text design by Sue Lamble
Typeset in Stone by MacGuru Ltd
info@macguru.org.uk

Printed in the UK by CPI Bookmarque, Croydon, CR0 4TD

For Aaron

Contents

About the author

Margot Katz is one of Britain's most successful business gurus and has worked across five continents with some of the world's leading companies, including BT, Chevron, CISCO, Coca-Cola, Reckitt Benckiser, Royal Bank of Scotland and Toyota.

Until 1997, she served as a director on the UK board of Ivax, a global pharmaceuticals company, where she played a pivotal role in its exponential growth under a visionary and entrepreneurial leader. She was instrumental in shaping and driving the people strategy that delivered substantial business results.

She moved into the consultancy arena in 2000, as head of consulting for DDI (UK), where she specialised in strategic leadership, executive coaching and leadership development.

She now works independently, and consults throughout Europe and beyond to Russia, India, Singapore, South Africa, Dubai and Argentina. She is a recognised and inspirational speaker on matters linked to the Tarzan and Jane themes in her book.

Born in South Africa, she now lives in North London with her husband. As you read the book, you'll discover that she supports Arsenal and enjoys a mellow merlot. And her middle name is Jane.

Foreword
by Neil Holloway

The future world of work

The combined impact of technology and globalisation over the past decade has created a much smaller world, often referred to as a 'flat' world, full of almost 'virtual' organisations that are always connected. Add to that intense competition and a total focus on the customer, and we are seeing an amazing impact on the world of work for organisations and individuals. We are being forced to rethink and to ask ourselves whether what we offer is unique. To thrive in an overloaded and competitive world we have to differentiate ourselves in better and better ways and I believe that our biggest differentiator is our people. It is critical therefore to attract the best people to work in our organisations whether they're 18, 35, or 50. As an employer, we face a huge challenge if we can't attract or retain great employees who reflect the diversity of the markets we serve.

If the Industrial Revolution was about muscle power, the trend in the Technology Revolution is more about information workers and brainpower. In this world the individual is king, and when the impact of an individual is so important a company needs diversity. I believe that innovation rises exponentially with diversity. For stand-out performance, we need people who think differently and have different ideas and different ways of working.

Moreover, today we are all personalising everything so we can stand out, whether it's through blogs, ring tones, clothes or cars; our music, our politics or our football teams. All say, 'I am me, this is what I stand for.'

And so, with this global, competitive world becoming more personalised, more customised and more concerned with the individual, both Tarzans and Janes have to know how to stand out by understanding their strengths and max-imising them. This book shows how anyone can do this.

Individuals: what do we need to do to thrive?

Tarzan and Jane uses 'people speak' rather than 'corporate speak' and its four themes resonate with me. We absolutely do have to understand our 'Inner Game' – to know what makes us tick and what we want to stand for – and it must be clear to others, too. If we know what we're 'Bloody Good' at, if we know our strengths, we can make conscious choices to max-imise ourselves and establish our brand. We must then make sure we amplify that message, or 'Turn Up The Volume', in the way that we communicate, recognising that it's important to know you're good and act that way without overplaying how good you are, which is seen as arrogance.

The fourth theme, 'Don't Just Sit There', is particularly interesting. As a company we can't 'sit there': our industry is too competitive. It's all about first to market, first to call, first to profit. Similarly, as an individual, be known for what you know. Information is the new currency. In the past, keeping it to yourself gave you power; now, sharing is much more socially acceptable. Be a 'go to' person, someone people turn to, and that way you'll always stand out.

Employers: what do we need to do to thrive?

It really is people that will make the difference. At my regular management updates, one of the four key areas I always focus on is our people. I look at succession plans, I look at our top 50 talent and I look at diversity and inclusion. These need to be a priority for all leaders. We need to be able to answer the employee question: 'Why should I work here?' I wake up every morning asking myself: 'How do I make this the best place for people to work'; 'How do we help them to realise their dreams and maximise their potential?' I also focus on the evolving culture shift we'll all need if we're to survive and that means a blend of both Jane's and Tarzan's ways of working to enable the shift towards greater teamwork. And that will bring more collaboration and empathy, with people reaching out to all those they engage with: colleagues, partners and customers.

How do we do all that? There are a few key things we should be focusing on:

- To start with, we need to hire smart people who are Bloody Good regardless of age, gender and race. Then we need to enable these great people to do their best work, making sure we help them to have great careers. It's important to remember that employees are customers too – they have a choice about where to take their talent.

- To keep people engaged, we need to ask them for feedback regularly and we must listen, understand and act. There is more buy-in from people that way and we'll know how to help them realise their full potential.

- There needs to be a vision of where people are going and they need to understand how they all connect to the vision and values. For this to work we need the right leaders to bring this alive and we need a lot of good role models. Unless we role model the values and make them very clear, people won't believe them.

- Lastly, we need accountability. Being clear about who is accountable is always tough because there are so many unclear boundaries and so much co-ownership of projects. Generally, leaders are not too good at holding people accountable, but we have to do it if we're to give people the clarity they need to thrive and deliver high performance

So, not only is *Tarzan and Jane* clearly relevant for individuals, but also leaders reading it should be thinking, 'Wow, that's how I need to work to build the workforce of the future', because the book is a great tool for exciting and engaging people with a fun new vocabulary, and the four themes apply pretty much all around the world.

Neil Holloway
President of Microsoft Europe,
Middle East and Africa (EMEA)

Neil leads Microsoft Corporation's business throughout EMEA, focusing on driving customer satisfaction, improving integration across Microsoft's business units, addressing the unique technology needs of diverse markets and growing the software business in the region. The region includes more than 15,000 employees serving 139 countries.

Introduction

*No problem can be solved from the same consciousness that
created it. We must learn to see the world anew.*

Albert Einstein

I believe that the role of business, taken in its broadest sense
of endeavour, is to make the world a better place. It generates wealth, offers choice and creates jobs. Work, whatever
we do, is hugely important to individuals, too. Way beyond
income, it provides us with opportunities for self-expression,
self-respect, self-fulfilment and opportunities to shine. So I'm
clear that it's worth taking your place in the corporate jungle
and making it your own.

What do Tarzan and Jane have to do with all that? This
book was conceived as *Me Jane* and was going to be about
helping women to thrive in the corporate jungle. I read all
the statistics and they convinced me that gender was still
a significant issue, with the workplace depicted as a hostile
environment where women are squashed by glass ceilings.
But, when it came to it, the more I talked to people about
their success, their hopes, their dreams and concerns, the less
I heard about gender. It just wasn't on anyone's radar. Men
seem to have their share of issues and to want different things
now: more time to wake up and smell the coffee. And those
women who wanted to be on top were. Reflecting on their
experiences and my own, I came to realise the real issue is
much more to do with being yourself and creating your own

distinctive brand, with gender difference as an enabler rather than a barrier: less about the divisions between 'he' and 'she'; more about 'me' and 'we'.

So the book became *Tarzan and Jane* and it's not about what governments and organisations ought to do. It is not about women having to fix themselves or having to become more masculine. It is not about men abdicating from the corporate playing fields of the future. It is about men and women adapting their styles to work together, and that's what will generate the new corporate jungle. It is all about women and men recognising what they want for themselves, recognising their own value, knowing what they stand for and what's important to them. It's about taking personal responsibility for change, and about being visible and self-expressed. It's about developing and flexing an authentic personal brand that broadcasts uniqueness. How does Jane get her message right when she's managing men – and women? Can she have power and femininity? Does she have to 'behave like a man' to be heard? How does Tarzan get his message right when he's leading upwardly mobile women, or serving powerful and wealthy female clients? How does he tone down his 'testosterone-driven' style and build up his 'emotional intelligence'?

By the way, it's worth mentioning up front that you don't have to be a woman to be a Jane or a man to be a Tarzan. Most of us are Tarzanes or Jazans, a healthy mix of both cultures. Jane is a man or woman using a predominantly female style, and Tarzan is a man or woman using a predominantly male style. *Tarzan and Jane* provides insights and practical solutions and answers some perennially knotty questions.

The answers come from the lessons I've learned and the people I've listened to, leading to a blueprint that has been created from the blood, sweat and tears of a very personal journey. The path laid out for you to follow is still warm.

The book is a cornucopia of ideas, research, quotes, stories, role models and practical steps to take to help you 'see the world anew' and to show you what to do with what you know.

Tarzan and Jane reveals the four themes of differentiation that make up your own personal brand and that provide a blueprint for success: The Inner Game; Be Bloody Good; Turn Up The Volume; and Don't Just Sit There.

- **Theme 1 The Inner Game** – reflecting on the aspirations, beliefs, values and passions that are right for you now

  This section is all about self-awareness and self-confidence. It asks particularly why there is such a lack of confidence in Janes. It encourages you to be in charge of yourself and to take responsibility for what you want to happen rather than finding reasons outside yourself or blaming others. As priorities are shifting for Tarzans and Janes, it asks: What do you want? What's important to you and what do you stand for? Is there a conflict between your values and the way you live your life? And how do you best combine children and career without feeling guilty? How are you stopping yourself from being who you want to be?

- **Theme 2 Be Bloody Good** – excelling at your craft and keeping ahead of the game

  Successful people are 'Bloody Good' at what they do. They know their strengths, focus on them and maximise them with creative development plans and a strong mentor. Tarzans and Janes bring different things to the party and the combination is powerful. This section also takes you through the art of communicating authentically and how to bridge gender differences. There is a need to understand the other culture, and neither be in awe of it, nor be contemptuous of it, but work within it.

● **Theme 3 Turn Up The Volume** – clarifying your personal brand in the age of the sound bite

This section is about Tarzans and Janes equally and invites you to articulate and express your own uniqueness and personal brand. It's about being a larger and crisper version of you – not about trying to be like someone else. Turning Up The Volume does not, of course, mean being rude or arrogant; there is a fine balance to be struck between being egotistical and being invisible. Rather, this section is a coaching lesson in getting your message across consistently in what you say, how you look and sound and in your body language. It's also about using considered, strong language to create a powerful impact.

● **Theme 4 Don't Just Sit There** – connecting with your market and getting known

Strategic networking, an essential ingredient of success, is hugely misunderstood and underutilised, and this applies to both Tarzans and Janes. Contrary to popular belief, it is not about using people and is not the exclusive domain of extroverts. It is all about connecting to people, building relationships and helping others without seeking a direct return, a style often natural for Janes.

Reflecting on these four themes is self-affirming and uplifting. The time is ripe and the future is rosy.

Introducing the role models

People tell me that there are never enough real, accessible role models and we need them; I've found eighteen great ones for you who provide good examples of what I've found more generally in all my experience in business. They're all high achievers at different levels, with very different aspirations and experiences, and meeting them has shaped and influenced my thinking. They provide wonderfully rich insights and inspiration, bringing the themes alive in their unique ways. They openly and honestly share not only their successes but also lessons learned from their mistakes, and in some cases, I talked to their colleagues to get a fuller perspective of them. They range from 25 to 50-something, are at various stages in their careers, and are from different functions and different sectors. You'll be meeting them as they weave their way in and out of the relevant themes. May I introduce you to:

Abigail Sharan, the woman with a circle of excellence
Abigail is responsible for partner strategy across Europe, Middle East and Africa in Microsoft's Information Worker Business Group. She received a Circle of Excellence Award for outstanding achievement and has been selected for the Talent Programme for future leaders after only eighteen months with Microsoft. And yet even she has had to overcome dips in confidence from time to time.

Adam Oliver, the man who attracts nice people
Adam leads BT's research into new technologies that help disabled and elderly customers, tackle climate change and create a more inclusive society. Adam has built his reputation on a quirky brand that makes him approachable, admired and memorable. He is a constant connector of nice people

Albert Ellis, the evolved accountant
Albert is CEO of Harvey Nash, a top-tier global firm of search and selection consultants. Albert, a former musician and accountant, is stamping his brand of values and empathy onto a typically hard-edged Tarzan environment and provides cutting-edge advice.

David Gold, the entrepreneurial philanthropist
David is CEO of ProspectUs, a specialist not-for-profit recruitment agency. David left a successful career as a board director

in the City to follow his passion and to live a life he loves. As well as running a thriving business, he has a high profile and is well known for the huge amount he does for his charities.

Debra Covey, the woman who moves mountains of people to do massive things

As managing director of BT Wholesale's Networks, Deb is responsible for all the operations in the UK for all the platforms where you see the BT brand. That means leading 10,000 people and overseeing a capital budget of around £1.3 billion. Hailing from Texas, Deb is a born leader with a forthright and direct approach, who thrives on huge, complex challenges.

Diana Boulter, the woman who speaks her mind

Diana founded and is CEO of DBA Speakers, a company which provides business and after dinner speakers for corporate and private clients. Diana, an enterprising entrepreneur, has built her business on the highest standards, on strong values and on her brand of refreshing honesty. She's a walking 'who's who' guide with boundless enthusiasm for what she does.

Dyfrig James, the Welshman who wears red socks

Dyfrig is managing director of the aggregates and concrete business of Lafarge in the UK. Lafarge is a worldwide leader in building materials, a business with annual revenues of £800 million. Dyfrig's personal brand is characterised by his large personality and his bright red socks. When you look deeper into his brand, you'll see that a passion for safety is at its core.

Gill Bruce, the intrepid adventurer

Gill is responsible for diversity and corporate responsibility at Coutts UK. Part of the women's initiative, her role is to attract women to the bank as clients in their own right. She has a reputation for her daring fundraising activities and brings a sense of adventure to whatever she does. She's a fun and generous networker.

Harry McGee, the man who got away

Harry is the chief operations officer of VADOS Systems, providers of voice and data-enabled technology. He grew up in a black ghetto in St Louis and has managed to create a successful life using the military as his passport out. He uses his determination, his talents and his faith to make sure he never goes back.

Keri Landau, the eventual public servant

Keri is employed by the London Borough of Lewisham as part of a team tasked with monitoring contracts of housing-related support services for client groups ranging from domestic violence to substance misuse. Still early in her career, she struggled to find her niche, but now her career in public service is rapidly taking off.

Lisa Fabian Lustigman, the class act

Lisa is a family lawyer at Withers LLP, a leading international law firm dedicated to the interests of successful people. Lisa advises her clients on all aspects of private family law, including divorce, with an emphasis on complex financial and children issues. Exuding New York style and confidence, she came to a career in law via theatrical aspirations in an unusually roundabout way.

Lucy McGee, the consummate juggler

Lucy is marketing director of OPP, a firm of consultants and business psychologists, famous around the world for their psychometric instruments. Lucy is someone who masters whatever she turns her hand to and shines. She's one of those women who have managed to have it all, combining a great job with being a great mother.

Mandy Ferguson, the chocoholic with a dream job

Mandy is managing director of Ryvita, famous for its rye crispbread. She's built her career in the food sector, including one particularly perfect job with a chocolate company. She's got to where she is as a result of her huge passion, talent and energy, and she works her socks off.

Noorzaman Rashid, the man with the little black book

Noorzaman leads the division at Harvey Nash responsible for headhunting executives for board level jobs, mainly in central and local government, health and education. An assistant CEO by the time he was 27, he is now extraordinarily well connected with over 3,000 CEOs as part of his network.

Roz Savage, the woman who rowed the Atlantic

Roz followed the expected path from Oxford to the City, where she spent eleven years trying to figure out what she really wanted to do. She couldn't have found a more extreme path and ended up rowing the Atlantic solo. She shares the many lessons she learned on the way.

Rukhsana Pervez, the 'sensible Sally'

Rukhsana is a regional manager, part of Chevron's Global Workforce Development team covering Europe, Africa, Middle East and Eurasia. She is the youngest regional manager to sit on the management team. She zaps all over the world, manages a team of six and is still only 31. Can this really be the male-dominated oil industry we're talking about?

Sarah Deaves, the passionate 'people's banker'

Sarah is CEO of Coutts Bank, the international private banking arm of the Royal Bank of Scotland Group, and manages assets for some 98,000 clients worldwide. Sarah is one of the few women to have risen to such heights in the banking world. Contrary to what you might expect, she's down-to-earth, practical and approachable

Trisha Watson, the woman who shared her job

Trisha is group marketing manager for the public sector at Microsoft. Trisha believes that we always have a choice and it's up to us to choose. And that's what she's done. A high achiever, she's made a decision to job share so she can spend more time with her young children and still have a great and meaningful job.

How to use this book

Put your future in good hands: your own. This book will almost become your own personal coach, on tap at all times to challenge your thinking and provide practical hints and tips for any stage in your career. Different themes will be more important to you at different times, and the book will be there to support you long after the first reading.

Here are four suggestions to help you to get the most out of this book:

1 'Cashmere socks'
Whenever I want to go into myself, dream a bit and think creatively, I get out of my office, cocoon myself somewhere cosy and put on my lovely comfortable cashmere socks (particularly wonderful in our cold British weather). The soft, warm feel of them instantly transports me to the zone-like state that allows me to quieten the inner voices and really hear the whispers and deeper thoughts that pop into my head. That's how I do my best thinking. You'll come across these moments in role model stories, described sometimes as an alpha state, an epiphany or a bolt from the blue. A cashmere-socks moment doesn't need socks at all and can be whatever takes your fancy – sitting in a garden, listening to music, walking in a field, having a massage or sipping your favourite wine somewhere special. You can even have one in the rush hour on a crowded underground train.

The rules for a cashmere-socks moment are simple: just let the thoughts flow and listen to them; don't analyse, don't censor, and don't dismiss things that are way out there.

2 Hippy groups

The hippy in me loves the idea of a self-help group. I know they sound decidedly un-British and very much a Jane thing, but have a go; you'll get so much support from working through the four themes with a few trusted people. You'll become confidants and advisers to each other and the results you'll get will be far greater than when working on your own. Peer support and challenge will drive up your commitment and determination to do what you said you would without resorting to a single stick of incense. Get together with a small group of colleagues (ideally up to six), draw up your ground rules, set your agenda, agree your modus operandi and watch how well you get on. If you're a leader, the four themes are a great tool for exciting and engaging your team, so encourage them to set up hippy groups to go through the journey together.

3 'Ah ha' books

When Roz Savage was rowing across the Atlantic, she learned many life-changing lessons which she stored as 'Ah ha' moments in her logbook. Begin your own version of this by capturing your thoughts, ideas, insights and action plans in one place as you go through the four themes. I have a penchant for gorgeous notebooks. I buy them in all colours, shapes and sizes; I select the smoothest paper and choose a pen that glides over the pages, so that the writing itself is a wonderful experience. Treat yourself to your own brand of book and keep it with you so you can capture random ideas as they pop into your head.

4 Making it stick

If you want to do something different, try something new, change something, take charge, then the steps that follow are what will bring it all alive for you and will transform your experience of reading the book from simply a 'good read' to life changing.

Anything is possible for you and the journey might be easier than you imagined. Of course it will take practice; learning theory that says that it takes about 1,000 hours to become consciously competent at something. There are already plenty of great things you're doing to be successful, so remember to keep the positives in sight.

What do I do?

1 Focus and plan

You can't work on everything right away, so prioritise. Decide what is the most important area to focus on and use the planning tools provided to stay focused.

2 Keep it going

It's easy to lose focus, to get discouraged, to forget the urgency, so you need to put some checks and balances in place. Here are the steps outlined in the section on frog goals to choose from:

- Create a process. Set your goals, take action, track and review your progress.
- Select a tracking mechanism. The important thing is to keep your goal alive.
- Declare it. Not 'losing face' is a driver for many. Having support from a mentor or a coach can work wonders for you and will increase your commitment.
- Use your hippy group. Peer support and pressure will drive up your accountability and determination to do what you said you would.
- Visualise it. 'Picture yourself winning,' as Harry Emerson Fosdick, an American Baptist minister, said, 'and that alone will contribute immeasurably to your success.'

- Build confidence and overcome self-doubt. To paraphrase Henry Ford's words, whether you think you can or whether you think you can't, you're right.

Armed with your soft cashmere socks and your smooth 'Ah ha' notebook, supported by your hippy group and the role models, you're ready to begin the journey. As George Eliot said, 'It's never too late to be what you might have been.'

The Inner Game

Overview

What lies behind us and what lies before us are tiny matters compared to what lies within us.

Oliver Wendell Holmes

When I think of what the Inner Game means to me, words like whole, authentic, grounded, 'liking yourself' come closest to describing what it feels like. The Inner Game reflects on the confidence, attitudes, beliefs, values and passions that deliver the right results for Tarzans and Janes. It specifically explores the thorny issue of how values and goals are woven around family commitments. It encourages you to be in charge of yourself and to take responsibility for what you want to happen rather than blaming others or finding reasons outside yourself; and this includes the glass ceilings that some Janes talk about. It asks: What do you want to achieve? What's important to you and what do you stand for? Is there a conflict between your values and the way you live your life? How are you stopping yourself from being who you want to be?

This section invites you to take the time to reflect and to update where you are. Once you understand yourself, everything else falls into place and makes sense and you are free to relate authentically to others.

And what's up for grabs is a sense of clarity, a renewed sense of purpose and direction and a silencing of the distracting self-talk that holds so many of us back.

These four steps build on each other, adding up to the whole Inner Game – the foundation on which all the other themes are built:

1 Bumblebee confidence
2 Frog goals
3 Life's too short to stuff a mushroom
4 Who's in charge?

Step 1: Bumblebee confidence

What's in it for me?

Limiting beliefs will always hold Tarzans and Janes back. Confidence and belief are essential ingredients in achieving anything: they're what enable you to fly.

Other people intuitively sense whether confidence is present or absent, and this will have an impact on how you are perceived.

The good news

Something can be done, whether you're a Tarzan or a Jane, because it's a mindset rather than a fixed condition: confidence can be built and beliefs can be updated.

What's it all about?

Did you know that according to any laws of aeronautics, the bumblebee shouldn't be able to get off the ground? Apparently, it is too heavy, its wings are too small, its body is too big and it doesn't have sufficient muscle. There is no way it should even get off the ground. The thing is, nobody told the bumblebee and it just carries on flying.

Some people have a bumblebee mentality and just expect things to work out for them. And guess what? They generally do. Condoleezza Rice, the American Secretary of State, is a bumblebee. She was brought up to believe in herself and was convinced that although she might not be able to have a hamburger at Woolworth's in Birmingham, Alabama, because of her colour, she could be president of the United States.

By the way, not one of my Jane role models considered a glass ceiling as they built their careers; like the bumblebee they took responsibility for themselves and got on with it.

You always know when confidence and belief are present. Take a look around at the people you know who have it in bucket loads. You'll see presence and strong posture: you'll witness clarity and decisiveness; you'll sense strength and energy. And you can always tell when it's not there. I'm always fascinated to watch how lack of belief affects sports performance. You just sense when someone is going to miss that penalty, or when a tennis match is going to be lost.

Abigail Sharan, a high performer with a high degree of self-assurance, describes a time when her confidence levels were lower than usual. Many will relate to her experience.

....

The woman with a circle of excellence

Congratulating Abigail Sharan for her recent Circle of Excellence Award for outstanding achievement, or praising her selection for the Talent Programme for future leaders after only eighteen months with Microsoft, you would be forgiven for thinking that it has all come naturally and has been effortless.

But in spite of being familiar with the company through a previous role as a successful consultant to Microsoft before joining the company, her first months in the new job were tough. 'I found myself in a Black Hole with no idea of how to get out,' she says. 'I couldn't see the wood for the trees and even though I had clear objectives, I couldn't figure out what I was supposed to be doing.

Even when I asked for help or advice, I didn't understand the answers. I knew people were speaking to me in English but there was so much jargon and the words were so American in style that I couldn't make out exactly what they were talking about. It didn't help that I had extremely high expectations of myself as did my boss, given the previous experience I had in working with Microsoft.'

She recalls a presentation she gave to business leaders early on in the black-hole days: 'I felt uncomfortable. I was nervous and I knew it was coming across in my tone of voice and body language. I used language such as "maybe" and "perhaps" instead of "this is what we should do". I was annoyed with myself. You know you can do it, you know it's inside, you know you have high self-belief so why aren't you showing what's inside?'

Abigail put herself under enormous pressure to prove that she was up to it. She overcompensated by working incredibly hard, and although getting through volumes of work, she ended up being incredibly stressed out. What she now realises is that she had to go through all of this, to figure out how to get through it so that she could move up to a new level with renewed confidence. It proved to be the making of her. She learned some life-changing lessons (which we'll see later in this theme) which have left her much more authoritative, poised, in control and self-assured. She now feels comfortable in her own skin and is doing things in a way that makes her feel positive while still delivering outstanding results. It feels genuine and authenticity seems to be what people notice and value.

....

Having confidence is a basic ingredient for success and well-being. Boosting your confidence will certainly improve your results and will make you feel a whole lot better in the process.

I continue to be astonished at the extraordinary lack of self-confidence in so many extraordinarily talented women. It just doesn't add up.

Consider this scenario. A company I was working with were looking to appoint someone to the board. They told me about what happened to the applications of two particular internal candidates, both of whom would be excellent. Of those two people, the first looked at the requirements and thought, 'Hmm. I only have 75% of what's needed; I guess I'm not ready', and didn't apply. The second thought, 'Great! I'm already 75% of the way there – I'll go for it!', and got the job. As you've guessed, the first person was a Jane and the second a Tarzan. Aware that she's generalising, Trisha Watson of Microsoft finds that men have a greater innate sense of career confidence that allows them to get on and progress. 'Many women don't set their sights high enough and need to be convinced they can do something before doing it: they are more risk averse,' she observes. There's plenty of evidence to suggest that women limit themselves in making personal career choices because of a lack of confidence and a sense that they will be 'found out' to be not really as good as people think. One piece of research compared 85 women and 255 men at the director or vice-president level and found that the only competency on which the women consistently scored lower than men is self-esteem.[1] Even among entrepreneurs, an area where women are enjoying enormous success, females say that lack of self-confidence is the biggest barrier to success.[2] This is not to say that men don't also suffer from a lack of confidence at times, but it is certainly less widespread.

I always remind myself that something can be done about this with the 'Tale of the Roast Beef'.

The Tale of the Roast Beef

A young couple were about to cook their first Sunday roast together. As they prepared the meal, she noticed that he cut off the ends of the joint of meat before putting it onto a dish and then into the oven. She'd never seen that particular technique before and, curious to learn more, asked, 'Why do you do that?' He explained that his mother taught him to cook that way, but he didn't know why it was a good way to cook roast beef. The following week they had the chance to find out. When they were visiting his mother they asked her why she cut off the ends of the roast beef before putting it in the oven. But they got no further in their quest to discover the secret. Her answer was pretty much the same as his; it was something her mother had always done.

Finally, they went to the source and asked grandmother to explain her culinary art. They put the same question to her, and asked her why she had always prepared her meat that way. Her answer was simple: 'When I learned to cook, my oven was very small and I had to cut the ends off the meat so it would fit in.'

....

Like the roast beef, sometimes our actions, beliefs, feelings and attitudes go way back; they may have once made sense but are no longer valid or useful today; and they can limit us and limit our confidence. For a start, we have far more inner resources and self-knowledge available now than when they were first formed, so it's time to do a reality check and see whether yours are affecting your confidence levels today.

How do I stack up?

Awareness is always a good first step, and you probably already have a pretty good sense of your levels of confidence and belief. Here are a few questions to help you gather your thoughts. Take a cashmere-socks moment and reflect.

- Self-talk: what do you say to yourself? Is it different at meetings; with your boss; at a job interview; with colleagues; with clients? Do you generally encourage yourself or generally talk yourself down?

- How proud are you of what you've achieved? Do you accept compliments about your work? Do you compliment yourself?

- Do you give yourself a hard time or forgive yourself when things go wrong or when you don't achieve the result you want?

- Do you hold back from applying for jobs, because you don't have 100% of the requirements?

- Do you express your views openly? Do you stick to them if others disagree? Are you willing to put your head over the parapet and stand out?

- What's the difference in your confidence levels when you are with people of your own gender?

- What state are you in physically (churning stomach, shaking knees, damp palms, relaxed, calm, comfortable) when: you enter a room full of strangers; make a presentation; go for a job interview?

- When you take on a new project, are you excited, assured or worried that you won't meet others' expectations?

- Do you assume you'll get what you want and that things will turn out just right?

- Do you feel that you are going to get 'found out'?

Are your reactions different in different circumstances? What's different when you react differently?

What do I do?

How do you build up self-confidence and belief? Based on my clients' favourites, here are my top five hints and tips. See which feel right for you.

1 Act 'as if'

If you act 'as if' you are confident now, you are more than halfway there. You are already in charge of your moods, feelings and states and so are in charge of changing them for more useful states at will. It's not that successful people don't lack confidence at times; it's more that they get over it, as Abigail

Sharan's story showed. The late Mo Mowlam recounted a time when, as a new Member of Parliament and full of fear, she was invited to address a group of city bankers knowing absolutely nothing about banking. She put on her best suit, and with her shoulders back she strode into the room and said in a firm manner, 'Gentlemen, very good to see you. Could you each give me five minutes on the major issues we should be addressing?' At the end of the highly successful lunch, she hadn't had to express a single view on anything and had conveyed absolute confidence.

Test it out for yourself.

- Choose a confident person as your role model – it can be anyone at all, living or dead, male or female, real or fictitious. It could even be you when you are feeling at your most fantastic.
- What does it really feel like to be that confident? Now really get into their skin and take on their body language. Imagine what it's really like and take on their confidence as if it's your own.

I used this early in my career when I had to make much dreaded and feared cold calls. I hated this part of my job with a passion. At the time, I had a friend, Sally, who loved selling, loved talking to people and had not a jot of my dread and fear. So, when making calls, I 'became' Sally. My facial expression changed, my voice changed, my energy level changed, my confidence changed and my success rate changed. It works.

Sometimes, just changing your physiology is enough to change your state. Feeling tired can be transformed by moving around; feeling low can be transformed by talking to someone; lacking confidence can be transformed by simply adopting grounded physiology – standing squarely with upright posture, shoulders back and breathing deeply from your diaphragm. This works well for Tarzans and Janes alike.

For Lisa Fabian Lustigman, the family lawyer from Withers, a favourite way to build confidence has always been to draw on her thespian inclinations, almost as if preparing for a role. And that's exactly how she prepared for one of her interviews. The 'role' demanded a confident, articulate person, so she rehearsed what she would say, how she would show that she knew her legal onions, and dressed the part in a classy, classic suit. She slowed her speech right down to mask any nerves; she kept herself calm with deep breaths and an open and straight posture. You can still see this authority in Lisa's bearing today. She thought of every possible killer question that might come up and prepared and rehearsed answers until they felt fluent and natural. She also prepared her mental state (like Mo Mowlam) in advance, thinking about the room, the people who would be there and how she would come across.

As you behave as if you are totally confident, you begin to believe it and become it. And it shows.

2 Use constructive self-talk

We all have a voice that runs in our heads all the time, a running commentary on everything that's happening. You may be thinking, 'Which little voice, I don't have a little voice, what's she talking about?' Well it's that one. It's also known as self-talk. Often our self-talk is less than helpful, letting us know that we're not good enough in some way. 'I can't do that.' 'They're much better than me.' 'I'll make a fool of myself. I might fail.' 'Can I do it?' It is this self-talk that gets in the way of our confidence levels, as we've already seen with Janes, so we all need to learn to get out of our own way. Instead of spending time wondering about whether we can do something, we should just get on and do it.

It works rather like this. Imagine a bucket filled to the brim with murky, stale water. Now imagine taking a large pebble and adding it to the water in the bucket. What happens? The water has to slop out to make room for the pebble; the pebble displaces the water. Imagine doing this with more and more pebbles until, finally, when you add enough pebbles, the murky water is totally replaced. If negative self-talk is like the murky water, it too can be replaced by constructive self-talk, the metaphorical pebbles.

The mind is only capable of one thought at a time, and if you are having a positive thought, there is no room for a negative one at the same time. So it makes sense to fill your mind with positive self-talk – life becomes much more fun. The old adage is true: if you say something enough times you believe it.

Here are some guidelines that go with creating constructive self-talk:

- **Express in the present tense.** 'I am' is far more powerful than 'I will be' or 'I could be,' both of which fail to motivate. They are too wishy-washy and too vague. 'I am OK' is more powerful than 'I will be OK'. When you are making affirmations about self-development, phrase them as if they are occurring now. For example, 'I am becoming more and more relaxed.'

- **Express in the positive – towards, rather than away from, something.** 'I am courageous' works better than saying 'I'm not afraid'. This is why. If I ask you not to think of a pink elephant, what happens? You think of a pink elephant, right? Thinking about what you don't want means you have to think about it in order not to. So it still lives in your mind as murky water; no pebble is displacing it.

- **No need to explain, or rationalise, or justify or say how you'll get there.** Keep them brief; these are not goals, they are just self-talk statements

- **Use language that stirs you.** There isn't a right choice of words, an ideal turn of phrase. Language of possibility is likely to be more stirring than language of necessity. 'I am making a real difference' is better than 'I need to do this or I ought to do this'.

- **Choose no more than five, because the mind cannot concentrate on too many.** Write down your top few, for example: I am confident; I know my stuff; I am valuable; I can do this; I make a real difference. Keep them handy and look at them often – they become more and more real.

My all time favourite is the L'Oréal strapline, 'Because I'm worth it'. What a perfect pebble. Something good happens in your body when you use constructive self-talk. For me, it's a warm squidgy feeling somewhere around the oesophagus.

Rukhsana Pervez of Chevron admits that she hasn't always felt as confident as she should; 'I can't be as good as they think I am' is the self-talk going on at these times. Her liberating moment came on a course she attended. Being presented with the latest theories and best practice governing organisational development, she saw clearly for the first time: 'But that's what I already do, I don't need to know the names of the gurus or the latest models – I know more than I think.' And with that came a wonderful sense of what she's achieved and how good she is. The old self-talk was way out of date and needed to be updated.

3 Look at things from a different perspective

Frida Kahlo, a Mexican artist, was involved in a bus accident in 1925 and suffered severe injuries to her body when a pole pierced her from the stomach to the pelvis. She drew a picture describing the event and you can see her lying on the ground, horribly injured. Watching the scene is her detached face, observing everything from outside her body. Without needing to be in such a dreadful situation, you can do the same and look at yourself from outside; it can be a great way to get a different perspective. When you're in any situation, become that face looking in and see how much more you can see. Roz Savage took herself outside herself when she was struggling to keep her spirits up in the middle of the Atlantic. When she was struggling – and boy it was hard going at times – she'd remind herself of Churchill's observation: 'When you're going through hell, keep going.' She would talk herself through it, imagining herself at the other end of the experience. 'It may not be a bunch of fun right now, but think of the fun it will be talking about it over a glass of bubbly with friends.' So she visualised a future dinner party as she learned to stand back from it all, almost to watch herself from afar, seeing herself from the outside. Stepping away from an experience allows you to be dispassionate, to have the perspective that it will pass and you will have learned from it.

Another way to get a different perspective is to redefine the situation and give it a different context, so you can relate to it differently. You can do this with anything or anyone that is causing you a problem. The imagination is such a powerful tool and so available to create a solution at any given moment, even a quick and temporary one. What do I mean? I was on a plane flying home after coaching someone in Stockholm. I ordered a glass of red wine and prepared to unwind and reflect on the day. Unfortunately, it was not to be; across the aisle from me was an irritating and screaming little girl. My usual response would have been to do a 'Victor Meldrew' and stew. But as I didn't fancy two hours of puffing and sighing, I decided to get over it instead. I made myself imagine that one day this irritating little girl might be a kind, brilliant and wonderful doctor – the very one to be looking after me in an hour of dire need. Strange, perhaps, but it did the trick, and the irritation disappeared in an instant. You can have fun with this, too. One of my clients had a bullying boss and felt diminished in her company. So he created an image of the boss as a very small and extremely fat toad, wearing a pink tutu and black Doc Martens. He just had to laugh, and having this image in his mind changed the impact his boss had on him when they met, and he was able to respond differently.

4 Prepare

People tell me that they never prepare enough. Noah did not start building the ark when it was already raining. Being well prepared is such a simple thing and earns you so much. It increases your confidence and the likelihood of success, which in turn builds more confidence. Whether it is a presentation, a meeting, an interview, knowing your stuff and rehearsing what you want to say, will make all the difference. In my experience, Janes in business tend to be more conscientious and better at preparation than Tarzans. Learning theory has it that it takes about 1,000 hours to become consciously competent at something and about 5,000 hours to get to the point where you don't even need to think about it – you're unconsciously competent.[3] Preparation moves you towards this level of performance.

Rukhsana Pervez is a consummate planner. From early on she is always thinking about her next steps, always has a plan, is always determined and always wanting more. 'I'm the sort of person who runs towards responsibility,' she explains. 'I like to be well prepared and one step ahead of the game.'

She tells me of an incident when she was to report back to a very senior team. She was under pressure for time, and relying on a surge of confidence, going against her gut, she decided to 'wing it' – so unlike her usual highly prepared approach. And it bombed. She faced a hostility she hadn't planned for or expected; and was rescued only by a mentor who believed in her and had the vision to see beyond the immediate situation. Afterwards, relying on her relationship-building skills and natural emotional intelligence, she followed up, not allowing things to be left ignored. She followed up with each person after the meeting, explaining her case, exploring their reactions and making a huge personal effort to rebuild bridges. It was a terrible experience and an invaluable lesson: always prepare and never wing it in a high-risk environment.

All performance excellence is built on practice, rehearsal and preparation, whether sports excellence, musical excellence, academic excellence or business excellence.

Here's a checklist for you to select from when preparing for anything.

Purpose
- What is the purpose?
- What is the outcome you want?
- How do you want people to feel afterwards?

Focus
- What are the issues?
- What do you need to know?
- What do you need to cover?

Target
- Who is your audience? What do you know about them?
- What do they know? What don't they know? What do they want to hear?
- What might they be feeling?
- What are their possible responses? What killer questions might they ask? How will you answer?

Practical stuff
- How much time do you have?
- What do you need to take?
- Where will it take place?
- Where will you sit? Will you stand?
- How will you convey your message? Do you need any visual cues or handouts?
- What will you wear?

Ending

● How will you close?

● What are the next steps?

Be a 'Noah', Tarzans particularly, and test this out by preparing thoroughly for the next big thing coming up and see how it boosts your effectiveness and your confidence. As you become practised, you'll be able to prepare quickly, perhaps rehearsing in your head on the way to the meeting.

5 Do a reality check

It is only human to sometimes feel less than great. Everyone has their moments of thinking they're just not up to it, not as good as others would be. We fear awful failure. To help with this, imagine a piece of paper, completely blank save for a single dot drawn in the middle. If you ask someone what they see, the response is always 'the dot'. But, if you think about it, the 'not dot' is a far greater area. Similarly, instead of concentrating on what's wrong, switch to the far greater number of things that are right. For example, instead of saying 'I'm indecisive', ask yourself, 'Aren't I more than indecisive? What else am I besides indecisive? And what else? And what else? And what else?', until you have a far more balanced sense of yourself.

Here's another reality check: separate your emotions from the reality of the current situation.

So put on your cashmere socks and organise your thoughts:

● What is the worst that can happen?

● What is likely to happen?

● What else might happen?

● What can I do to positively affect the outcome?

● How do others see my abilities?

● What am I already good at? And where have I already succeeded at something similar?

● What do I choose to think about myself instead?

Conclusion

By now you, especially Janes, have had the chance to understand more about your own confidence and self-belief, have worked through the top tips for upping your game and discovered your inner bumblebee, like Condoleezza Rice.

The next stage in the Inner Game is to focus on what you really want. Having direction brings purpose, energy and passion.

Step 2: Frog goals

What's in it for me?

Knowing what you want will give you vision and focus, a sense of purpose and direction, confidence, energy and passion. And these in turn will transform your results; remember it's you who gets to say how far or fast you want to go. Going beyond your comfort zone can be hugely exciting. People accomplish great things once they've given themselves permission.

The good news

We all have goals in many areas of our lives: working towards a holiday, a new car, moving home, becoming healthy. So the good news is that the art of goal setting is likely to come naturally and you probably already have processes in place for achieving what you want. My experience has been that people get what they focus on, so having your goal in mind means that you're well on your way to achieving it. Then it's all about focus, planning, visualisation, belief, using that bumblebee confidence and sticking with it.

What's it all about?

Imagine a great game of football. There is so much energy, focus, passion and competitiveness. The players work like crazy, running up and down the pitch with an unwavering drive to win – sustained right until the closing seconds of injury time. Now imagine the same game, but this time, take away the goal posts. With no goal scoring, what's left? Energy without purpose, a game with no point – you'd soon see the energy and enthusiasm drain away.

This section invites you to explore your goals and clarify what you want and where you're heading. It encourages you to define what's right for you: not what your parents want, your boss wants, your children want, your partner wants, your friends want. The expectations and traditions are often different for Tarzans and Janes, but the process is the same for both. It's time to question what is relevant to your own life now. The other key word is want. Not ought, not should, not might, not perhaps, but what you want. So this section creates an opportunity for you to consider the choices you have made inviting you to explore new possibilities and widen your options.

Frog goals

There's a story about a frog that sat at the bottom of its well and looked up to the sky. What it saw was a beautiful circle of blue sky, which made it so very happy. It was only when the frog climbed up and up to the top of the well and looked up again that it saw how much bigger and more marvellous the sky really was. Like that frog, we may be seeing only a small part of what's possible. But if we get ourselves to the top of the well, we will have an entirely different view of what's out there.

Having a frog goal means looking at what's beyond the comfort zone and perhaps choosing some unsafe options. Roz Savage went from a small sky life and made a massive shift. Somewhere uncomfortable is where she ended up.

The woman who rowed the Atlantic – I

'In 1984, when I was 16, I was already planning how to organise babysitting for the New Year's Eve of the millennium. I was that much of a forward planner and I just assumed I'd be doing the conventional thing – married with children – by then.' Instead, by 2000 the bottom-of-the-well life with its familiar goals was being shed and Roz Savage was embarking on unimagined adventures of frog-like proportions. So what happened?

Roz, a graduate of Thatcher's Britain, knew she was expected to go straight from Oxford into the City as a management consultant or investment banker. With parental approval firmly behind her, she embarked on a career at Accenture. As she put on her pinstripe suit and sensible shoes that first day, she felt inauthentic, as if she were dressing up in grown-up clothes and putting on an act. She knew even then that this was not for her but reckoned it would do as a stopgap until she figured out what she really wanted to do.

Eleven years later she was still doing the same thing, still at the bottom of the well, still uncertain what she wanted to do with her life. Each morning as she stood on the platform waiting for her train, she would be overwhelmed with a desire to run in the opposite direction. But for eleven years she didn't. Born to Methodist parents, her modus operandi was a sense of duty, thinking she had to do the right things, and a sense of having to please others. 'I actually think this is a common theme with women,' she reflects.

As a child she spent some time in the USA where she was encouraged to believe that you can be anything you want to be; a frog at the top of the well, in fact. This was a very different outlook for her and it was this belief that eventually led her to make a move. With a paradigm shift from right inside, she realised that she needed to be totally free, free from all constraints and free from the treadmill created by having a high mortgage. Her frog goal, the idea to row the Atlantic, hit her from way off left field, a bolt from the blue. She believes that when setting goals you need to get into a reflective 'alpha state' to allow your unconscious mind to get a word in edgeways, allowing you to think beyond your usual constraints.

Roz's 'alpha state' is like cashmere-socks thinking and is a good way to go about reflecting on what you want. It makes bolts from the blue possible. When we get into the planning side of goals, we'll take a look at how Roz went about preparing her voyage. Clearly, few of us will decide to row the Atlantic, and frankly I can't think of many things I'd like to do less. But we'll have our own version of the Atlantic to row. Many of us get into things as a result of expectations, and unless we question and revisit our decisions we will remain at the bottom of the well.

How do I stack up?

Before moving to some frog thinking, it's worth checking where you are.

On a scale of 1 (low) to 10 (high):

- How passionate are you about what you're doing?
- How close is it to your dreams?
- When have you stepped up and used frog thinking?
- When have you missed opportunities to do some frog thinking?
- What has held you back so far? List all the reasons. Is that all?
- How far has your gender affected your choices?

What do I do?

1 What do you want?

Different things hold us back. It can be a fear of failure, believing we can't. Nelson Mandela spoke of this in his inaugural speech in 1994, quoting Marianne Williamson. He describes it as a fear of being 'powerful beyond measure', particularly among Janes that makes us play small, so that other people won't feel insecure around us. It can be uncertainty about what exactly it is that we want. Or we may just be too comfortable to go for something more. At one of my seminars a woman working at the Royal Bank of Scotland (RBS) Group came to realise that though she had accomplished much in her early career, she had stopped setting goals, stopped stretching and feeling alive and purposeful. She set about this next exercise with renewed vigour. The questions will help you to think beyond what might be limiting you and will give you a hand up as you climb to the top of the well.

This is definitely a cashmere-socks moment. Put everything to one side for a few moments and curl up somewhere really comfortable, well away from any distractions, and allow yourself to reflect on these questions, remembering Walt Disney's words: 'If you can dream it, you can do it.'

1 If you didn't have to answer to anyone, what would you do? ('Anyone' can include a bank, your partner, family, or your boss.)

2 If there were absolutely no chance that you could possibly fail, what would you do? Put another way, if success were guaranteed, what would you do?

3 If you won the lottery and money was no longer an issue, what would you do? (Okay, after clearing the mortgage and taking the world cruise, then what would you do?)

4 Imagine yourself up on a stage being presented with an award. What's the award for? What have you contributed that has made such a difference?

5 How big do you dare to be?

6 'Second Life' is a 3-D virtual world where you can create an entirely new identity and a new life. What identity and life would you choose?

Now take a look at your answers. Do any themes emerge? Are you being a frog? Do the answers give you a clear sense of what you want? Have you had a 'sail the Atlantic' moment? If so, you can move straight into the planning stage. For some, it's not as simple as that. There are no clear answers, just vague wishes. Things are in the way; there are practical considerations and we just can't clear the mortgage or leave our kids to sail off into the sunset.

But this can be a great time to start making changes and getting more of your wishes to become goals so you can get focused on them.

- Is it time to move job?
- Is it time to do more with your present job?
- Is it time to do some financial planning?
- Is it time for a salary increase?
- Is it time to commute less?
- Is it time to travel more?
- Is it time to update your image?
- Is it time to make time for relationships?
- Is it time to improve your health?
- Is it time to learn something new?
- Is it time to have more fun?

In my experience, getting started might be easier than you think and it's just a matter of fine-tuning or getting organised to make sure you're on the right path. A friend once told me, 'If I won the lottery, I'd get a personal trainer and I'd get fit.' Then he laughed at the ridiculousness of it; you don't need lottery millions for that. With a little juggling and organising, with a few phone calls, he found his trainer and began.

2 Focus and plan

I love this part; it's so practical and energising. You can't work on everything right away, so prioritise your goals: what's the most important, what gives you the greatest buzz, what will make the greatest impact, what's the most urgent? Here's how it works for Abigail Sharan of Microsoft. Realising that she was taking on way too much in order to prove herself in her new job, Abigail took stock. To help her prioritise, she worked out what legacy she wanted to leave behind when she left this role and focused on what would best deliver it. This was inspiring and energising, helping her to focus on the right things and allowing her to make decisions about what she would or wouldn't do. She was then able to spend more time focusing on the important things. She created her personal 'rules of engagement': no working at weekends; reducing travel time where appropriate using conference calls and web meetings instead; days to work from home; getting to the gym. Work suddenly became manageable and she had the right levels of energy and well-being to forge ahead. The fire in her belly and her competitive nature mean she is often drawn to taking on more; she now tries hard to pull herself back. Learning to set expectations with the people she works with is also really important.

People respond differently to goals. Some prefer huge frog goals that stretch and excite them; others prefer to start small and build confidence incrementally. Know what works best for you. When breaking down the biggest goals, start with the end in mind, as Stephen Covey advises,[4] and work back from then to now with all the steps and stages in between. Small successes build confidence and form a basis of belief for the bigger challenges. Select your primary goal or goals, making sure they enthuse and inspire you.

However large or small your goal, make sure it is SMART – that is, Specific, Measurable, Achievable, Realistic and Timed. But there's one extra element: define everything in the positive.

Here's the SMART+ checklist for creating achievable outcomes:

- **Define your outcome in the positive**
  Ask what you do want rather than what you don't
  want. For example, 'I want to be on the mergers and

acquisitions project team', rather than 'I don't want to be left behind'. By the way, losing weight and giving up smoking are negative outcomes and often difficult to achieve; try out instead the goal of becoming healthy.

- **Specific**

  Know exactly what it is. 'I want a holiday' is too vague. What are the specifics? I want to go away at Christmas, somewhere that will be hot, a twelve-hour maximum flight, somewhere I can speak English, where I won't have jet lag and which won't cost me more than £2,000. You'll probably find yourself setting off for South Africa.

- **Measurable**

  Define how you will know that you're on track, that you're succeeding. What will the measures be? Feedback or a tangible result like a pay increase, an increase in revenue, a purchase made, a project plan completed on budget and in time? How will you differentiate between acceptable and outstanding performance? What does outstanding look like?

- **Achievable**

  Do you have the resources you will need and will you have access to them? Resources include things, time, people, money and your own personal skills. Build confidence and belief. Ask yourself: Why will I be good at this? What have I done before that is similar? Who will help me? What self-talk will help me? What beliefs and states will be most useful? What time and effort will this goal need? What will I need to give up and am I prepared to do it? Who else might be affected by my going for this? What impact will it have on them? Am I and are they comfortable that the impact is acceptable? What is good about the status quo? What do I want to keep?

● **Realistic**
Is this within your control? Is it too stretching? Can it be done? What are the contingency plans if something goes wrong? How will I keep myself on track? What milestones do I need?

● **Timed**
When will you do this? When do you want it? Deadlines provide huge impetus. The football game demands that all is accomplished within a set timeframe and that focuses and drives the players.

3 Keep it going

It's easy to lose focus, to get discouraged, to forget the urgency, so you need to put some checks and balances in place. Here are a few ideas that work well. Choose what's best for you.

● Create a process. Whether you're running a project, working on your performance plan, or setting goals, you'll use pretty much the same process. Set your goals, take action, track progress, review progress and evaluate. In evaluating, it's good to adopt an attitude that there is no failure only feedback and learning; sometimes, good things come out of what appears at the time to be a disaster. When something goes wrong, make yourself say, 'I'm glad this happened, because…' Even if you don't get it at the time, there always is a 'because'. So encourage yourself and recognise when it's time to change direction or move on.

● Select a tracking mechanism. People use Gantt charts (a graph to show the length of each project against the progression of time), diaries, to-do lists, project planning sheets and Microsoft Outlook. Use whatever tracking mechanism you prefer, but the important thing is to keep your goal alive. Remember to reward and praise yourself en route.

- Declare it. Telling people what you're up to puts some tension in the system: not 'losing face' is a driver for many. The support of a mentor or a coach can work wonders and will increase your commitment.

- Use your hippy group. Peer support and pressure will drive up your accountability and determination to do what you said you would.

- Visualise it. 'Picture yourself winning,' as Harry Emerson Fosdick said, 'and that alone will contribute immeasurably to your success, but picture yourself losing and that alone will make victory impossible.' Sports people visualise the medal or the finishing line to motivate them through their training. See yourself on the podium delivering your presentation confidently while you're researching and preparing. See yourself after you have accomplished the goal: Where will you be? Who will you be talking to? How will you be feeling?

- Use your bumblebee thinking to build confidence and belief and overcome self-doubt. To paraphrase Henry Ford's words, whether you think you can or whether you think you can't, you're right.

Setting out to row the Atlantic, Roz Savage was naturally using many of these ideas.

....

The woman who rowed the Atlantic – II

Roz Savage met someone who had rowed the Atlantic with his mother. She thought, 'If his mother can do it, then I can most certainly do it.' Still she went through many wobbles during her preparation, doubting herself, trying to talk herself out of it. 'It's a ridiculous idea, much too big, much too challenging.' But it was so completely perfect for her, so right in so many ways, and that feeling kept her going when she felt daunted or overwhelmed.

She set about getting prepared: she had to learn about weather and navigation; she had to build up her physical strength. It was a huge learning curve. She geared herself up to getting to the starting line, but it was much actually harder after the starting line because only then did she begin to learn her life-changing lessons. For a start she learned about having the right objectives. She never intended to win any race; she simply wanted to prove that she could organise and execute a row across the Atlantic, and to find out what she was capable of when there was nobody for hundreds of miles around to offer help. Looking at the others involved, you would have expected the only woman rowing solo for the first time to come in behind the men and the rowing teams. But when she did come in last, she berated herself: 'I gave myself a really hard time thinking that I had not performed. I learned that I had to judge my performance against my own aims and not be sidetracked by what others are up to.'

She's learned that a life spent trying to please others is a life doomed to failure and frustration. It's best to focus on what you're trying to achieve; the best objectives are the ones you can control. And it's much better to set achievable goals. 'I planned to row for sixteen hours each day, and that wasn't realistic. As it happened, I only rowed for around twelve hours and felt a failure. How ridiculous: twelve hours is massive by any standards. I should certainly have set a stretching and huge goal, but it also should have been achievable. Then I would have been patting myself on the back and feeling confident, instead of beating myself up.'

Was it all worth it? She found something she passionately wanted to do. 'Heart and head, body and soul, everything was in alignment. It took a huge leap of faith for me to dare to live my dream, to start living the life I believed I deserved.'

....

Choosing what you want, then going for it step by step with the right mechanisms and support in place is the way to get you to where you want to be.

'Crazy paving' career paths

The goal setting we have looked at so far is structured and specific, and works with a future vision and works backward. There's an alternative approach to goal setting that is more fluid and open. It works by focusing energetically and rigorously on the present and meandering forward, taking opportunities as they arise without specifically seeking them out. I call this approach 'crazy paving' planning and it's particularly relevant to career paths. Sir Dominic Cadbury, a member of the Cadbury chocolate manufacturing dynasty, once said: 'There is no such thing as a career path. It is a crazy paving and you have to lay it yourself.'

I must admit, for a long time I thought that all people who were successful in their careers applied frog thinking, something like 'I'll be managing director by the time I'm 35', and then set about achieving it single-mindedly. I came to realise that it's often not like that at all. Few of the role models I interviewed knew what they wanted from the outset: Lisa Fabian Lustigman, the successful family lawyer, wanted to be the world's greatest theatrical star; Mandy Ferguson, managing director of Ryvita, thought her only options were to be a secretary, nurse or teacher; Albert Ellis never imagined he'd end up as CEO of Harvey Nash when he set out as a musician. The progress of their careers was exactly like crazy paving, evolving slab by slab. And sometimes it took a while to get where they wanted to be. Consider this crazy paving story.

....

The class act

Lisa Fabian Lustigman's story is inspiring because her path was not the typical route to success in the law.

The only child of two prominent New York psychiatrists, she defiantly set off for London aspiring to be the world's greatest theatrical star. While waiting to be discovered, she turned her hand to selling advertising space for a tabloid newspaper. Hating every minute of it, and slowly recognising how unlikely success in the theatre would be, she knew she had to take control of her life and made the decision to be a lawyer. Her path to qualification was rather like undertaking the labours of Hercules. She failed exams, she passed exams and she had four children, including twins, on the way. At the age of 35, she was still immersed in mother and toddler coffee mornings, while her fellow students were already long qualified. She needed to get qualified and realised she was hardly an appealing candidate. As luck would have it, the father of her son's best friend was a solicitor in a small firm and after an informal interview she joined them and qualified.

For the next fifteen years, family came first and she worked part-time, her feet growing roots under the desk. But as time wore on, she gradually moved apart from the ethos of the firm, and realised that it was time to move on, out of her comfort zone.

She became the new head of family law and a partner at a prestigious firm. She thrived, going from strength to strength, building her reputation and expertise with each case. This time, it was a merger that motivated her next move. There was a place for Lisa within the newly formed firm and she was encouraged to stay, but in a lesser role. By this time, she had enough confidence in her abilities to know that she didn't need to opt for second best for no good reason. 'I wanted to do something different for the swansong of my career. I wanted to stand on the shoulders of giants, and to know that I could make it within the magic circle of the very best firms.' Her network led her to one such firm, Withers, a leading international law firm dedicated to the interests of successful people, one of the very best. There Lisa advises her clients on complex financial, property, children and jurisdictional issues. Partnership is not an option, nor is it an issue for her. She simply wants to be doing an outstanding job, surrounded and stimulated by the best and brightest minds.

....

Being responsible for her choices and laying slabs along the zigzagging path at least five times has taken Lisa to exactly where she wanted to be each time. Many others, faced with similar hurdles, are still languishing and waiting for something to happen to make things better for them.

Conclusion

Not only are you a bumblebee, you're now also a frog who has climbed out of a well and is beginning to feel pretty good. The next stage in the Inner Game is to reflect on your values, what's important to you. As Roy Disney, the younger brother of Walt Disney, said, 'It's hard not to make decisions when you know what your values are.'

Step 3: Life's too short to stuff a mushroom[5]

What's in it for me?

Having your values foremost in your mind will give you the inner strength that comes from knowing what you stand for; it will help make decisions and, as the heading suggests, will keep you focused on important things which may or may not be stuffed mushrooms. What's most important to you should never be sacrificed by focusing on things that matter least. Your confidence, goals and values are the foundation for your passion.

The good news

Whether you're consciously aware of your values or not, they're probably already there and guiding your life. This section is about raising your awareness of them and clarifying them for you to use as guiding principles. There are no 'oughts' or 'wrongs' when it comes to values – they are what they are.

What's it all about?

I remember once working with my colleagues on the board towards a massive company-wide SAP implementation. (SAP is a company that specialises in technology-based business processes and solutions.) I was under enormous pressure; deadlines were due, project leaders were screaming and there simply weren't enough hours available to get everything done on time. In the midst of it all, a friend's mother died and the funeral was being held at the time of an important project meeting. I didn't know what to do and called my husband to talk it through with him. His advice was the best I've ever had and has stuck with me ever since. 'Go with your values,' he said, 'and you'll know what to do.'

I went to the funeral. And did the work get done? Of course it did. Am I still with the company? No. Do I still have the friend? Yes.

We all have core values, which are meaningful and personal. Values are not necessarily logical and we can't always explain them using reason. Values are why we do what we do, what's important to us. The stuffed mushroom is simply a metaphor to highlight the importance of focusing on what really matters. And stuffing mushrooms may be very important, especially if you love preparing beautiful meals.

This section invites you to check out your values; to align them with your goals and with the values of your place of work. When I reflected on the stories of the role models, I could see how much they were guided by their values as they made important decisions. This came out in the different choices Janes made about balancing career and children, and in the career choices Tarzans made. Different things are important to us as our priorities change during our lives, so it's good to take stock from time to time.

Here's the story of a role model who has made profound career decisions based on his values and is now living a values-led life.

....

The entrepreneurial philanthropist

When I met David Gold for this interview, in the early autumn of 2006, he had just returned from an eight-week summer holiday with his family to celebrate his fiftieth birthday. 'But you know,' he smiles, 'I was just as happy to be back at work as I was to be away. For me, there is no work–life balance, just my life. I'm lucky. I have enormous fun and enjoy everything I do.'

David spent much of his first successful career at Philips & Drew, where he demonstrated his flair for fund management and equities, so much that he was promoted to the board after just twelve years. Volunteering, helping young people with disabilities has always been important to him, and he continued while thriving in the City. He was bowled over, finding wisdom and maturity in people fighting adversity. He tells of the time when, breaking all the rules, he ran very fast down Shepherd's Bush Road pushing someone in their wheelchair, giving them the experience of a huge adrenalin rush. Volunteering always helped him to put organisational behaviour into context. 'People get so caught up in things that are relatively unimportant,' he observes.

After some years in the City and still enjoying himself, he had a bolt-from-the-blue moment at a board strategy meeting. He had a moment of vivid clarity and knew in that instant that he would leave: he wanted a different future doing valuable work of a different kind. His values of fairness, trust and integrity and his desire to help people drew David to the not-for-profit sector. Serendipity led him to discover a small business for sale, and he bought into ProspectUs in 2000.

The company, as you would expect, is founded on David's passion for people. All his employees are encouraged to volunteer; they are encouraged to work in an autonomous way. So with a strong and proactive team around him who share his values, David is able to spend an increasing amount of time on other things, also really important to him, particularly his own many charitable activities. He runs Glimmer of Hope UK; is chair of Philanthropy UK; is a director of Futurebuilders, a UK government initiative; and is a keynote speaker on philanthropy, often billed as the 'entrepreneurial philanthropist'. Living his values is what has him happy with his life.

David told me about the school of the Benedictine monks of Ampleforth, who with their wonderfully inspired thinking encourage their pupils to start writing their own obituary from an early age. It sounds odd, but this does get them to think about creating the life they want to lead very early on and provides a valuable context for their actions and decisions. Have you ever wondered what your obituary would say?

How do I stack up?

1 *What are my values?*

There are all sorts of ways to do this, but I like this simple way best. Look at the following list of value categories:

- family
- friends
- me
- career
- money
- health
- spirituality
- community
- the planet.

Which of these are not important to you and should not be on your list? What has not been included and should be added on?

The fact that there are so few women leading organisations may be nothing to do with glass ceilings; we've seen that there are enough women who want to, who are. It may well sit right here in values and what's important to you. If the majority of women seem content not to be top dog at the office as well as at home, it's much more likely that it's because they've weighed things up and don't want to be.

2   What's my driving value?

Look at your values and ask yourself, honestly, 'How would I rank these?' List them in descending order, or create a pie chart with slices sized relative to importance, remembering that they are all important to you.

You won't need that judging little inner voice that offers unhelpful comments and opinions: 'Of course you should put your children first; what kind of parent doesn't?' or 'You should be more focused on money – put it higher up' or 'You can't put work the lowest, what would your boss think of you?' Focus instead on what is true for you. One of my clients was ashamed that he'd put 'Me' as his first value, thinking that this meant he was self-centred. When we unpicked what it meant to him, he saw that without paying attention to his health, his well-being, his self-expression, he would not have anything to give anyone else – like the instruction on a plane to put on your own oxygen mask before helping others.

Children versus careers

This is exactly where this thorny subject sits, because it is a massive jostling of important values. It is so high on people's agenda that it is worth spending some time on it. Juggling work with the demands of raising a family is a fact of life and something millions of families contend with, some better than others. Childcare is increasingly a shared responsibility, where there are two parents. New Tarzans are to be seen at the school gate and at sports day, and are dab hands in the kitchen, though most Janes still see childcare as primarily their responsibility. There is a glut of popular novels where the heroine foolishly attempts to hold down a job while raising a family and fails miserably. Usually seeing the error of her ways, she leaves the job to start a hobby business. And in doing so, she becomes whole. While that is certainly one option, many of the Jane role models I meet fare better at the balancing act, though no one pretends this is easy. Clearly adoring their children, they also recognise that they need their work to stay sane. 'I'd be a bitch from hell, if I didn't work' is how one woman delicately put it. Only you can determine what's right for you and then it's up to you to make it work. You can have it all, but remember that having it all doesn't necessarily mean having equal time for everything.

Here are three stories showing one full-time Jane and two part-time alternatives that work well. Deb Covey has always worked full time; Trisha Watson is experimenting with a job share; Lucy McGee has made sure she found a great job near home and negotiated a part-time arrangement.

The consummate juggler

Seeing Lucy McGee talking about leadership on TV is like watching the proverbial duck swimming. It all looks so effortlessly professional, she performs so smoothly, but under the water it's a different story.

On a good day, Lucy McGee has it all: gorgeous husband, beautiful children, stunning job, stylish home, with good looks and a huge dog thrown in for good measure. On a bad day, it doesn't feel worth the massive effort it takes to pull it off.

Committed to her career, she and her husband agreed upfront on how they wanted to parent – no nannies and no boarding schools, these were non-negotiables for them. When her boys were small, Lucy had a stretching job, travelling and working full on. She met all her targets, earned her stripes but was downright knackered. It was more than she could cope with. Loath to lose her, her boss and HR were keen to find a workable solution and met her terms.

The result? An office-based marketing job and a four-day week. She had masses of autonomy and chunky projects. Her Fridays off gave her headspace, like the air between layers in a vacuum flask. She could exercise, catch up on admin, sort out the house and get the shopping out of the way, so that when the boys came home on Friday afternoon she was in the home zone, completely theirs and 'in the moment'. And this is still the pattern today. The weekends are always a work-free, chore-free time for the whole family. They watch TV, play, chill, talk and eat together: it's a time to cherish. Social life has sometimes been sacrificed but it's worth it.

Now for the nitty gritty – how does she organise her time? At the beginning of each month, the McGees sit down with their diaries and co-ordinate travel so that one of them is always home. Lucy, generally a techno laggard, was one of the first internet food shoppers – shopping is always done late at night after the boys are in bed as are other household tasks. 'I'd rather change the bed linen at midnight during the week than leave it for the weekend.' As for childcare, the early years were covered by one childminder, the wonderful Mary, so the boys had continuity and Mary's unbeatable sausage casserole. As they grew up, Lucy felt it was important for them to come to their own home after school, so the au pair stage began and this has worked well for them.

....

Momentary guilt is there for Lucy as it is for so many. But ultimately, she realises that she couldn't have been a better parent. She can't imagine feeling the same about herself if she hadn't gone for a meaningful career; she's had so much freedom, self-affirmation and spending money through work. 'Being at home more would have made me unhappy and horribly introvert. Stressful as it's clearly been at times,' she claims, 'I'd have been a miserable old witch hag if I hadn't.' One of the lessons she's learned is not to overcompensate the children through misplaced guilt. The temptation is to take them to expensive restaurants and lavish toys on them, whereas in reality what they remember is picking conkers with you in the park.

Different people need different solutions to suit their lifestyles and aspirations. Trisha Watson has found a different solution for now.

....

The woman who shared a job

'Knowing what's right, what's comfortable is an amazing place to be,' reflects Trisha Watson. 'It's all about choice and it's up to you to choose.' She's made the decision to job share so she can spend more time with her children and still have a great and meaningful job. She once compared herself to Nicola Horlick, who managed a top City job while raising five children, and she wondered whether she was less of a success for not doing that. She's found her answer. 'No. There isn't just one path and you can still make a difference.'

Trisha has always worked hard. An engineer, with a first-class honours degree, she was always focused, always striving, always achieving, until one day she sat down and thought, 'How much time have you actually given your kids? Is this what you really want?' She recalls a defining moment: she arrived home late one evening. Her daughter was already asleep and her homework was lying open on the table. Trisha saw errors that needed correcting but was leaving too early next morning to be able to help beyond hurtling through the door on her way out shouting 'there are mistakes'. She felt awful and realised that she had a choice to make.

It so happened that someone else within Microsoft in the UK was looking for a job-share partner. Trisha, with her mantra 'achieve, achieve, achieve', found the concept difficult to accept. Would it mean losing control? Would it mean she'd be in a role she wouldn't like? Would she be seen as less committed, less hard working? She realised that for it to work well, it would depend primarily on her and her job-share partner. It also helped that her team and key stakeholders within the business were signed on and supportive. Have they got it totally right? No, of course not. But there is the opportunity for honest feedback all round and for open dialogue at all levels which means that issues are ironed out quickly. She describes it as 'work in progress'.

For the individuals, is it what it's cracked up to be? What are the sacrifices? Trisha believes she truly has work–life balance; she has time for herself, time for her children, time for other projects and time for her great job. The only sacrifice has been salary, and that has been worth it for now.

....

Trisha is aware that many people still need convincing that job sharers aren't 'checked out', less committed, in some way. Job sharing, where one full-time job is split between two people, is becoming increasingly popular and increasing numbers of companies are starting to offer it. Look, for instance, at the employment policies of Asda, HSBC, KPMG, the BBC and PricewaterhouseCoopers. For an organisation, the benefits are clear: retention of talent, cover and succession, two brains to tap into. Research on job sharing by Barbara Oaff[6] found that job sharers score highly on their ability to lead, to solve problems and to remain resilient in the face of a setback. Perhaps, more significantly, it also found that most of them are outperforming their full-time colleagues in terms of output. More organisations should be doing more of this and it's not just a Jane thing. There are all sorts of reasons why men and women might want to job share that may be nothing to do with children.

As CEO, Sarah Deaves is keen to do things differently for Tarzans and Janes at Coutts and to explore different options, such as compressed hours or flexible working: 'The search for and retention of talent is key; as one element I must develop alternative ways of working. We need to be creative so that the bank can keep great people. There is a huge cost associated with the loss of productivity experienced in having to recruit and train up replacements.' She is pragmatic and knows you don't ever get it completely right, but she believes that with give and take you get far more from people.

The way that job sharing works in practice will vary from company to company and from job to job,[7] but this is how it works for Trisha. Her job-share partner works four short days and Trisha works three days, each being flexible and willing to cover for each other when needed. They sit down with their manager at the beginning of the year and look at their commitments together. To avoid confusion, it's all pretty well defined with clear demarcation lines. They decide who will take the lead on particular aspects of the role and who will take the lead managing different people in the team. They have their performance reviews separately and are measured separately; along the way they mentor and support each other. Their teams have the right level of support from both, and even though they may not be around every day, neither are most other leaders. It is a solution that seems to be working for them and is slowly gaining popularity with others too. According to a Labour Force Survey in 2004, of all women employees, 8.5% had a term-time working arrangement and 1.8% were job sharing. Unsurprisingly, the comparable figures for men were much lower. Only 1.6% of male employees had a term-time working arrangement and 0.2% were job sharing.

It may be a great option, but what if it's not right for me? What if part-time working is not a viable option? What if I can't afford an au pair or nanny? What if I'm a single parent? No one is saying this is easy, but there are solutions to be found. The government is always being challenged on child-care arrangements and in time these may improve. For now, these are some of the methods that I've used myself or have been chosen by people that I work with:

- childminders
- nanny/au pair share
- after-school clubs

- family – nothing quite like a grandparent if you're lucky enough to have one around
- shared lift schemes with friends
- Tarzan stays at home/works from home
- Jane stays at home/works from home
- self-employment, where you get to define your working times and patterns
- choosing a company with family friendly policies
- boarding schools – different and certainly expensive, but a viable option nevertheless.

There must be other ways that you've come across too.

Deb Covey has managed to combine a huge full-time career with raising her family by sharing the responsibility with her husband.

The woman who moves mountains of people to do massive things – I

Deb Covey started her family when she was 23 and had two sons by the time she was 26. She remembers how she sobbed in the car all the way to work on her first day back after having her first baby, thinking, 'This is so hard.' So, if you want to 'have it all', you've got to work hard to make it work and you must love what you do. But Deb is clear that if there's a choice to be made, it must always be family first.

Here's how she made it work. Her days were long: up early in the morning to gather and sort out the family; off to work; then dinner; then time spent with the family; and after the children went to bed she set about doing more work. It made for a very long, but very rewarding day; a day where all the boxes on her trade-mark lists can be ticked. For a goal-oriented person, this is hugely rewarding even if exhausting. From time to time, she'd have a mini meltdown or setback when she would need to reset, back off and re-gather herself.

A full partnership with her then husband meant the responsibility was shared. As both worked, they sorted out each day who'd be home first, who'd do dinner, who'd be on call. Deb often needed to travel but she never had to worry about the children; her husband was very good at everything. The only thing he didn't get right was the clothes, so as a 'control-freak mom' she prepared co-ordinated, matching sets of clothes for each day before her business trip, determined that she would not be seen as a negligent mother with neglected children in unmatched outfits.

Whatever it took, even while busy making a name for herself at work, she never missed a birthday or a major school event.

She was headhunted and made the decision to come to the UK in 2003 – a huge decision since she'd never been to the UK before – and her sons, then aged 18 and 21, remained at home. After lengthy discussions, they agreed as a family that if she was going to do something crazy, then this was the time to do it. Contrary to the perception that she had 'abandoned her family', she speaks to her boys every day and visits around seven times a year. It's been good for them to become more independent and eye-opening for them to discover the UK. And they're enormously proud of their mom and what she's achieved.

....

Now, back to you and your other values.

Each of your values in turn has a subset of values, which say what is important about them to you. Let's look at one value; you can do the same for the others yourself.

3   *What are my work values?*

Take a blank page, set a timer for three minutes and write down what's important to you in your work. Write down whatever comes into your mind, without censoring or analysing. Here are some examples that other people have come up with:

● achievement

- recognition
- fun
- learning
- people
- autonomy
- informality
- challenge
- making a difference
- money
- integrity
- trust
- creativity
- support.

Choose your top six and rank them.

Here's an example of an entrepreneur who has built a business based on her core work values of fun, integrity, honesty, directness, excellence and people.

....

The woman who speaks her mind

Diana Boulter weaves her way comfortably among the movers and shakers who populate her world. Her diary reads like a 'who's who': meeting with Dame Stella Rimington; call Sir Digby Jones; reschedule a date for Dame Betty Boothroyd; book Martin Johnson. Sitting beneath a picture of Audrey Hepburn in her office with its bright pink walls, wearing a bright turquoise jacket, she sums up her work. 'What do I do?' she laughs. 'Well, it's a bit like a dating agency, but without the sex.'

Her story is as colourful as her appearance.

Looking for a PA role early on in her career, an advert in the *Guardian* caught her eye quite by chance: 'Communicator with exceptional skills required.' It was a plum role with a fat salary, so she went for it. Despite a woeful typing test – 26 words per minute with double the number of errors was hardly stand-out performance – she was put forward. Her interviewer was a slick, upper class,

Jermyn-Street clad representative of the boss for whom she'd be working. She was offered the post. She thinks that it was because she was straightforward, honest and completely herself. She discovered that she'd be working for the high-profile 7th Marquis of Bristol. Diana had read stories of his drug taking in the press and with her strong Christian values she disapproved. So she made her position clear at the outset. 'If I see anything illegal from you or your guests, I will report you to the police,' she declared. He knew what she stood for and came to trust her. His sharp business acumen, his kindness and generosity were unfortunately masked much of the time, his brain befuddled by drugs. His vulnerability made him lean on Diana as his trust grew. When Diana decided to leave, there were tears all round. But she needed to move so she could regain a life of her own. Working with the marquis during this time she had no relationships, no time for church, no stability and as engrossing as it had been, it was time to move on.

With her skills now ingrained – organising brilliantly, looking after people, influencing, building trust – she was perfectly pitched for her next and current career: providing speakers for corporate and private clients. Her strong values permeate the way she conducts her business, so that with each encounter you experience her clarity, directness and honesty (she'll soon tell you if you're being too vague), focus, integrity and rigour, the highest standards, impeccable attention to detail and her warm interest.

....

Values are why we do what we do; they are what are important to us and we've seen how much their values have guided choices that the role models have made. You've taken stock of your values, reflected on your driving value and honed in on your work values; now it's time to consider whether your values are aligned with your frog goals and with the values of your organisation.

What do I do?

1 Are my goals and values aligned?

There can be a mismatch between goals and values. For instance, you may have a goal to go for an international role to get to the next level, but time with family is a driving value for now. You might want to work part time and develop hobbies, but when it comes to it, money is more important to you.

Consider these questions to check for alignment:

- What time and effort will this goal need? What will I need to give up and am I prepared to do it? Do I want to 'stuff mushrooms' or not? Lucy McGee was willing to sacrifice some social life; David Gold was willing to sacrifice his City career.

- Who else might be affected by my going for this? What impact will it have on them? Am I and are they comfortable that the impact is acceptable? For Noorzaman Rashid, the man with the little black book, his charity work and networking activities are so important to him that even though they have cost him precious time with his family, for him it's been the right balance.

- What is good about the status quo? What do I want to keep? Even a bad habit has upsides; smoking might give you time to relax that you want to keep when pursuing your goal to become healthy. Your current level at work might make you feel liked by others; do you want to keep this when you follow your goal of promotion?

A word about stress and health

One of the values frequently sacrificed on the altar of success is health. We rush from adrenalin rush to adrenalin rush; we lean on caffeine, alcohol and nicotine to see us through; we feast on junk food and famine on exercise. We rarely have time to just 'be'. Even holidays are no longer sacrosanct with ever-present BlackBerries and mobile phones.

Consider Diana Boulter's salutary tale. A few years ago, she was driving in the outside lane of the A316 near Twickenham when she suddenly knew she was seriously ill. With her head on the steering wheel, she switched on her emergency lights and waved her hand out of the window, signalling for help. Luckily for her, one woman took action and came to her aid, not letting up until she had managed to get Diana safely into an ambulance.

What had gone wrong? The diagnosis was a gall bladder that had gone ballistic, the result of many years of stress, and she is lucky to be here. It was an important lesson.

Now she tries to recognise the early symptoms of stress and deal with them, but she admits she's not good at this and this is still work in progress for her. She tends to keep going and keep going, until she's exhausted. One solution has been to take more time off to recharge her batteries, whether to have a pampering facial, to do her charity work or to work on the children's book she's writing.

I'm a firm follower of the 'Me Time' school of thinking and an ardent practitioner: bubble baths, football, candles, retail therapy, learning, volunteering, reading, chocolates, films, exercise, sleeping, good food, whatever it takes. Taking care of yourself will make you way more effective and feel a whole lot better. What can you give up or rearrange that would mean you can pamper yourself?

And a word about guilt

In the world of work, Janes are particularly good at guilt, especially when it comes to combining work and children. Guilt shows up when there's an unresolved inner conflict, perhaps wanting to do something but feeling you ought to be doing something else. The upside of feeling guilty is that it provides a clue that you need to take a look at what's going on. That's what the stuffed mushroom work is all about: separating what's important from what's not. The downside of feeling guilty is that it doesn't solve anything or actually get you anywhere, but once you've taken a good look at your values and goals, you won't need your guilt any more. Recognise that it's just noise in your head stopping you from being wholehearted about what you're doing. Learn to say a fond farewell to it. That's what Mandy Ferguson, managing director of Ryvita, has done. As a working mum with a career on a trajectory, her natural high energy enabled her to do a million things. The thought of not working fills her with horror: 'I'd be bored to death. I love work – I have to love it because I sacrifice so much time: I do it for me.' Guilt isn't in her vocabulary. She owns her responsibility: 'Those are the choices I've made.' She has made sure it works well, but she's clear that if push came to shove, her decision would always be her children over her work.

Deb Covey, managing director of BT Networks, has this advice for working mothers, based on what she's learned herself the hard way:

● Never apologise for the way you live your life.

● Don't overcompensate your children through the guilt of being a working mother; it's not good for them or you.

● Look at how much your family gain by what you do; you're a role model for them.

2   Do my values align with those of my role and company?

If your organisation espouses values that are at odds with yours, or if your job doesn't meet your criteria of what's important, you're likely to feel out of tune with those around you, uncomfortable and less than happy. This can affect your authenticity, your performance and your well-being. So it's worth taking stock and checking how lined up you are:

- Check your values against those needed for your current role. How closely are they matched?
  - Are you getting enough of your work values fulfilled?
  - Is there enough fun or challenge or meaning or money or recognition to satisfy you?
- Check your values against those of the organisation where you work and those of your colleagues.
  - Are you a person with high integrity working with 'sharks in suits'?
  - Are you a creative person in a company that doesn't value innovation?
  - Are you an undervalued Jane in a jungle of old-style Tarzans?
  - Are you a Tarzan surrounded by Alpha females?

When all is aligned passion, energy and excitement can rise to the surface, and you're likely to love your work. Listening to Mandy Ferguson describe her career, you see this in abundance.

The chocoholic with a dream job

Mandy was 28 when she began working for United Biscuits, her move the result of an ex-colleague's recommendation. The culture there suited Mandy. It was non-hierarchical, fun and rewarding, and she got to work with great people. With so many opportunities and such a close match of values, Mandy stayed with the group for fifteen years and loved it.

It took her just fifteen months to accomplish the objectives in her first job and she was eager for a new challenge. A corridor conversation led to a wonderful new job, made in heaven for a chocoholic, with Terry's, a company within the group. She adored this job and would have stayed for longer but the company was sold on to Kraft Foods and for personal reasons she could not relocate.

Mandy reflects that having a passion for your work makes a big difference, and she loves so much about her work. 'Marketers are sad people,' she says. 'We go round supermarket shelves, stroking our products and getting the hugest buzz when we see people buying them.' She loves making things happen, making decisions and taking risks. She's good at leading teams and getting people to do well. She loves being the catalyst for something taking shape and growing, always needing to feel that she's making a difference. She's wired for action, driven by the desire to change things for the better. And she's always worked her socks off.

Mandy has become more and more ambitious, energetic and passionate as she's gone on. She's grown in confidence through her experience. She came to realise that she was up to and wanted a managing director role. The Ryvita job ticked all her boxes: it was a managing director role, the right size, independent, on two sites and international. And the job fulfils all her work values: a perfect combination of people, challenge, variety, achievement and making a difference. She set to work in April 2005. She's ambitious for the company and has made significant investments that sing out her vision of a growing, dynamic organisation. People feel they're part of a business going places as she leads the brand away from dieting to overall healthy eating. She's working her socks off again, passionate about accomplishing what she has set out to do. As long as she keeps meeting her values – positive relationships with people, setting and overcoming challenges, making sure that her work is hugely varied and meaningful – she'll continue to make a difference and be passionate, energetic and excited.

Conclusion

Being clear about your values and aligning them with your life, your work and your goals gives the greatest foundation of all for confidence and fulfilment, for passion and purpose. When you find work that fuels your passion and has meaning for you, 'therein lies your voice', Goethe believed. Being clear is an important part of being authentic and being authentic is the foundation for good working relationships between Tarzans and Janes.

The final step in the Inner Game is about taking responsibility for yourself, and therein lies your power.

Step 4: Who's in charge?

What's in it for me?

Taking charge gives you power and choice. When you accept responsibility for something, your thinking shifts, your energy shifts and your results shift. Being 'poor me' leaves you passive and stuck or treading water.

The good news

You are allowed to be human – you don't have to be totally in charge all the time. You can still indulge in a little light social moaning, which can be enjoyable at times and does no harm. But you have to be aware of what you're doing and to know when it's not good for you – this section will show you how. Being aware means you get to actively and consciously make a choice about what you're going to do or what you're not going to do, and when.

What's it all about?

I stopped to buy a *Big Issue* in Covent Garden one dull, grey day. While I was rummaging in my bag to find £1.50, the vendor, Steve Foad-Elliott, began chatting to me. He was bright, cheerful and articulate. We talked about life, the universe and everything and I was struck by his full-on approach, his positive view of life and his lack of self-pity. Steve was clearly in charge of his attitude and it showed in his passion, wisdom and engagement. I left the encounter feeling uplifted and energised, the richer of the two for having met. I think of him often, particularly if I find myself moaning about something trivial.

The polar opposite is the person with the mindset of 'poor me'[8], a victim. Things happen to them; they are defined by things around them and rarely in charge of their own life; they wait for a fairy godmother or winning lottery ticket to save them. We are 'poor me' ourselves every time we say: 'it's my boss's fault'; or 'the company doesn't encourage me, that's why I haven't done it'; or 'I can't achieve my results because of the market.' Or how about this one: 'I can't progress because there's a glass ceiling.' Trisha Watson of Microsoft comments that although both engineering and IT are male-dominated, she never expected barriers to her progress because she was a woman, and she never encountered them. 'How you perceive something is often how it is mirrored back: if you don't perceive it as an issue, then maybe it isn't,' she reflects. Other role models, Tarzans too, were of a similar mind.

The law of cause and effect says that things that happen have a cause, which results in an effect. When you think that something or someone other than you causes the things that happen in your life – 'he made me' or 'it just happens to me all the time' – you have no power to effect changes. This section will show you how to be that cause, or 'in charge'; how to get results, not give reasons and excuses. There is a continuum between being completely in charge and completely 'poor me'. This section will also show where you are on the continuum so you can choose how to get where you want to be.

My favourite extreme example of being in charge is Mahatma Gandhi, who urged people to 'be the change you want to see in the world'. He held his ground, and from a position of non-violence inspired generations, shook an empire and sparked off a revolution, which was to change the face of Africa and Asia.

The next role model got himself out of a way of life that wasn't good for him and made his own success.

....

The man who got away

Harry McGee, known always as McGee, was born in Memphis to a couple who had a passionate but short-lived fling. His mother was married, had twelve other children and didn't want the burden of an extra child to take care of. His father reluctantly agreed to raise him, but the relationship deteriorated as his father became more and more abusive towards McGee. His prime bond was actually with his father's father, with whom he had a wonderful, loving relationship. When he was eleven, his grandfather suffered a stroke, was paralysed and could no longer support him or protect him from his abusive father. McGee knew he had to take charge of his life and get out. As a thirteen-year-old, his options were limited, so he decided to go north to St Louis, to try his luck with his mother.

He found himself in the middle of a desperate black ghetto where drug abuse and crime were rife. His mother was indifferent to him, though willing to accommodate him since he did, at least, bring another welfare cheque with him. Focused solely on survival in this environment, McGee knew that, once more, he had to take charge and find a way out. His chosen route was to get into the US military via a trade school. McGee worked hard and achieved good enough grades to get into the air force. He embarked on his training, left his family behind and was out of the ghetto. Despite the success he achieved, McGee was always driven by fear of the abyss that he had left behind, always determined to make his mark and keep moving ahead. He spent eight years in the military, doing just that.

Despite the security the military gave him, after eight years McGee took the plunge and moved into a civilian job and enjoyed a meteoric rise within the US civil service. He eventually moved to the UK, left the civil service and began his career in the private sector, which has led him to his current role as operations director at VADOS Systems. Financial security, and the material comfort it has brought, has been a lasting driver, reminding him that he need never slide back into the abyss.

Throughout his journey from the ghetto and beyond, he has never played the victim role, never been 'poor me'. He has taken responsibility for his life, sustained by his faith and his self-confidence, knowing that ultimately he can always count on himself.

....

Taking charge is all about taking action to get somewhere better without waiting for someone to do it for you.

How do I stack up?

Mark where you consider yourself to be on the continuum between each of the extremes listed in Table 1.

Table 1 ● Where are you on the continuum?

Being in charge	Poor me
Know what I want	Don't know what I want
Use time well	Waste time
Authentic	Put up a good front
Control my feelings	Controlled by my feelings
In control of my results	Not getting what I want
Have choice	No choice
Want to do	Have to do
Improving myself	Judging others
Results	Reasons
Yes	Yes, but
Take responsibility	Blame others
Praise and encourage myself	Give myself a hard time
Do what is right for me	Do what will please others
Change circumstances	Circumstances change you
Opportunity	Glass ceiling

Where you are on the continuum is not fixed: it changes in different circumstances. But are you comfortable with the general balance? What do you learn about yourself from these questions?

Here's the story of someone who chose to do what was right for her. She took responsibility to improve herself and be in control of her results very early in her career.

The eventual public servant

Keri Landau is 25 years old and sits across the table from me with a self-assurance and poise that belie her age. She is making her mark confidently in the public sector jungle yet her path has not been smooth, her journey not without confusion and false starts. From archaeology to anthropology, from Sheffield to south London, she had to discover what was right for her and take responsibility for her choices.

Good at school and a high achiever, Keri did the expected thing and went to university. But as soon as she started, she knew she didn't want to be there. Thinking it would make a difference she switched subjects, but this did not put an end to her malaise and she remained unhappy and disengaged. 'I didn't know why I was there,' she explains. Stickability was what she expected of herself. 'I've got to do it,' she told herself, until she chose to listen to a different voice that said, 'Who says? Actually, I don't have to do it.' She realised then that she did have a choice, took responsibility and decided to leave. People described this as dropping out. Keri says, 'On the contrary, it was a positive and brave decision not to be somewhere any more.'

She rescued herself from the unhappiest five months of her life when she left but was then faced with the challenge of having to justify herself and find something else to do. Not one to wallow, she took charge again and threw herself into the first job she could find, helping out in a health food café; she ended up as the manager and stayed for a year. During that year, with plenty of support from friends and family, Keri thought hard about what she wanted to do until she found the perfect thing: a degree in anthropology and communication studies. She took action and got herself accepted on the course. She had found her niche, loved the course and got a first class degree. Now, wanting to make a difference and help make society better, she's chosen to work in the public sector. It suits her and, eager to learn, she can see that she can carve a fascinating career for herself. She loves the working style and the quality of life, and sees how many opportunities for women there are. Many in Keri's position have sat back and wallowed in 'poor me'. She has taken charge, taken action and is already reaping her rewards and satisfaction.

Keri advises her friends, uncertain about what to do, to 'just get a job, do anything; you'll learn, earn money and something will come out of it'. If you don't know where to start, take action and just do something. You'll be moving away from 'poor me' with each step.

....

What do I do?

The key to empowering yourself is to put yourself in charge of the things that happen to you. Here are some tips to help you do that.

1 As if

Pick an area where you would like to be more in charge or less 'poor me'. Now act 'as if' you are, totally, 100% responsible for what is happening. Try on the belief that no one else has one iota of responsibility – it is all down to you. It doesn't matter whether it is true or not that you are the cause of the problem, but acting 'as if' you were will give you options and choices to change things. You won't get anywhere if you are stuck at 'poor me'.

Start a list and write down what's different and what's possible for you now. Add to your list as you go through these next questions.

Abigail Sharan took responsibility for her dip in confidence, and used this 'as if' technique for shifting. A couple of coaching sessions gave her some confidence boosters that serve her well. Her special favourite is what she calls her 'magic bracelet', which she described as follows:

> Think of a time when you feel confident, proud of
> yourself and notice what's different: what's the self-talk,
> what's the body language, what's the feeling, what's the
> breathing.

Get into that feeling and imagine yourself stepping into a magic circle that expands and magnifies that feeling a hundred-fold.

Allow the feeling to engulf you and you'll notice how you feel on top of the world.

Now capture that feeling in an image, a sound, a feeling so that you can recreate it at any time.

Abigail captured her feeling in the image of a bracelet, which she 'wears' around her wrist. That feeling of confidence is now accessible at any moment. On reflection, Abigail came to see that she was responsible for her feelings and actions while in what she calls the 'black hole' and could choose to get out of the cycle whenever she wanted to. That knowledge brings freedom and power.

2 Blaming and judging

I love watching the soaps for brilliant blaming. Martin Fowler, speaking to his *EastEnders* mum, is deeply stuck in 'poor me': 'She left because of you; it's all your fault. I'll never forget and I'll never forgive.'

When you blame others when things go wrong, ask yourself:

- How is my behaviour contributing to the problem?
- What am I going to do about it?
- What can I do to make this different?
- What else can I do, besides blame?
- When have I made a mistake?
- When have I done something similar or comparable?
- How would I like to be treated?

Here's a way to diminish the feeling: ham it up. This is how to do it:[9]

● Get a blank piece of paper and set the timer for about half an hour. Pick a situation where you're stuck deep in blame. Now write your version of the story that says how the other person is wrong. Write down everything they've done, in great detail, '... and another thing' – make sure you get that down, too. Give vent to all your feelings: rage, frustration, hurt. Just get everything out of you and onto the paper.

● Find a partner, someone you are completely comfortable with, or you can do this in one of your hippy group sessions. Read what you've written out loud to them. Ham it up. Get into soap mode and really be dramatic: 'Do you know what? It was always me who had to get the coffee. Can you believe it? No wonder things have turned out this way!'

Now read it again. Partners, your instructions are to act really bored as you listen to this soap story.

Now read it again ... and again.

By this time even you will be bored with the story and its power will have diminished. In doing this exercise, I don't mean to discount things that you feel deeply and are important to you. But it is so good to be able to laugh at ourselves, to send ourselves up. Seeing yourself as the star of a soap opera will help you to shift. I used this exercise to get over a difficult business relationship once and it took at least six iterations until I could move on. But I did move on without looking back; and the issue did disappear. In future, your hippy group can let you know when you're off doing your dramatic number.

3   What's my pay off?

For someone like Mr Skimpole in Dickens's *Bleak House* there is little incentive to take charge because the advantages of being irresponsible are so huge: he gets to be totally taken care of, everything is paid for and his problems are solved by others. It has been said that all human behaviour has a purpose, so the next questions to ask are:

- What's the purpose of my behaviour?
- What's in it for me?
- What's my pay-off for not taking charge?
- How will I take care of these benefits when I move on and take charge?

4 Heroes

I like to pick a few exceptional people as my metaphors for being in charge – people like Mandela, Gandhi and Mother Teresa. Think of your heroes, role models or champions:

- Would they act in this way?
- How would they act?
- Would the things that are stopping you have stopped someone like Mandela?
- Have a picture of them handy to instantly and wordlessly nudge you away from being 'poor me'?

5 Prepare to choose

Like the *Big Issue* vendor, we choose our attitude. There is no master puppeteer controlling us. We control our reactions however automatic they may seem. We choose to yell or count to ten; we choose to laugh or cry; to smile or frown; to be impatient or kind; we choose to feel sorry for ourselves or laugh at ourselves. Stephen Covey describes this as the space between stimulus and response in which lie our freedom and power to choose our responses.[10]

Think of a situation where you wish you had acted differently.

- What would you rather have done?
- What triggered the response?

● How could you have delayed the response to give you
time to select an alternative?

Now imagine a similar situation in the future. Do you see
yourself feeling and acting differently because you prepared?
What's the difference in the response that you get?

Allow time ahead of challenging circumstances to prepare
yourself.

6   Explanations, reasons and excuses

We have a hundred and one reasons to explain why we haven't
done something. The computer crashed; the bus was late; my
dog died; it was the 'wrong kind of snow'. As Samuel Johnson
says, we must 'clear our minds of can't'. We are masters at
protesting about what we can't do or why we didn't do it,
when what we're really doing is convincing ourselves until we
almost believe our own rhetoric. It puts a gloss of legitimacy
on our failure to deliver.

Don't look for reasons why you can't or explain why not:
say what you will do and by when. Anticipate problems and
communicate before they become unpleasant surprises. In
this context, it is worth noting that, according to research by
Pat Heim in 1992, men and women often talk about success
and failure in different terms.[11] When men succeed, they are
likely to attribute success to intrinsic factors, such as skills
and talents, and claim it for themselves. Failures are usually
beyond their control, for instance the computer fouled up,
or they didn't get the information they needed. Women are
just the opposite, often attributing their successes to outside
factors such as effort, ease of task or just plain luck. A woman
is also more likely to take personal ownership for failures.

7   The two degrees

Do we take responsibility for everything? Is everything equally
important? There's a limit to our energy and our appetite for
change, so it's important to prioritise, to know where we

need to be in charge and what we can comfortably live with. You can think about your 'poor me' behaviour in categories weighted by the degree of significance and the impact they have on your life. The first degree of moaning is light 'poor me' and is about things you can comfortably live with. The second degree is more visceral and is where your focus for change should be.

- **First degree.** This is the light recreational moaning, which can be quite enjoyable at times and does no harm. Moaning about the weather, the boss, the systems, the company and other generalised and light-hearted things is something most of us enjoy doing if we are not really too bothered about the issues.

- **Second degree.** If, however, you have a strong opinion about what the company is doing, and are personally affected and frustrated by the relationship with your boss, then these become a higher priority for you and mean you need to consider what to do. It's worth noting that 'bitchiness' or malicious gossip can hurt others and is not the same as light-hearted fun. Second degree things affect your career and have the most impact on your life: stress leading to ill-health; not getting the promotions, results or recognition that you need from your work; unhappiness; not seeing enough of your family.

Asking yourself which degree you are at will determine the urgency of your need to take charge.

Trisha Watson, of Microsoft, found herself in the second degree early on in her career and needed to do something. She recognises now that she didn't have the confidence to move when she should have. She found herself thinking that she didn't have a choice and in her mind her horizons were limited. 'Too many people stay in the wrong environment through perceived lack of choice,' she observes. One reason for this, she reckons, is that 70–80% of people move because of a poor relationship with their boss; and if things are not going well, your confidence levels are often lower than they should be. Therefore understanding yourself early is really important if you're going to take responsibility for yourself. 'If your boss isn't giving you the support you need, you need to find another way of getting it,' Trisha urges. She came through her difficult time by talking to her close network of friends and colleagues, 'trusted advisers'. This helped her get another view on things; the people who know you well can help you know yourself and restore the sense of confidence and perspective you need to move on. Trisha realised she didn't have the inner resources to take action, so she took responsibility for getting the support she needed. This built her confidence and she was then in the right frame of mind to take charge and move on.

8 *Giving yourself a hard time*

Giving ourselves a hard time when we get things wrong is to have a 'poor me' mindset – on the effect side of the continuum – and is particularly common in Janes. In taking responsibility for your situation, just do it and don't then spend time punishing yourself. A few years ago I went on a pitch for new business with a male colleague. We had prepared well but hadn't anticipated the client's questions or concerns and didn't get the business. I felt bad and went over and over and over what we could have done, what we should have done. My colleague shrugged and said, 'It's just one of those things – win some, lose some.' I found his attitude refreshing and I realised what heavy weather I was making of things. This incident taught me that Janes need to 'get over it' and Tarzans need to think a little more deeply about what's to be learned from mistakes.

Rukhsana Pervez, of Chevron, has a tendency to be a true Jane. Her best-laid plans have been known to fail. When this has happened, she has been hard on herself, berated herself and blamed herself for not getting the results she expected of herself. She's learned not to do that because it isn't constructive. If you are being judgemental about yourself, stop. Here's what you can do instead:

- Think of someone supportive, one of your fans, and ask what they would say about you.

- If you were parenting children who were being hard on themselves, how would you nurture them, reassure them and build their confidence? Parent yourself with the same words and metaphorical hugs.

- Sometimes things are just hard. Acknowledge what's hard and difficult for you; own it and encourage yourself through it.

Conclusion

Being in charge is enormously empowering. It's about not playing 'helpless' and not about playing the blaming game. It's about assuming responsibility for your own life and not attributing a false authority to others or outside factors.

The Inner Game: conclusion

Thinking about the Inner Game as a whole, it's about bumblebee confidence, frog goals and crazy paving career paths; it's about stuffed mushrooms and being in charge – not being 'poor me', waiting to be rescued. Together these form the foundation of all the other themes. Liking and valuing yourself, knowing what you want, what's important to you and what you stand for, and taking ownership for your career is a pretty good place to be. These apply equally to Tarzans and Janes. Without them in place, the other themes have a hollow feel to them. With them in place, amazing things come to us. The hippy in me believes in the magic and abundance of the universe. As Goethe supposedly said:

> The moment you definitely commit yourself, then providence moves. All sorts of things occur that would never otherwise have occurred ... which you could never have dreamed would come your way. Whatever you can do, or dream you can, begin it. Boldness has genius, power and magic in it.

What do I do now?

As you went through the exercises and read about the role models, as you took cashmere-socks moments of reflective thinking, you will have absorbed and integrated some of your insights already so you need take no further conscious action on those.

- Reread the Making it stick section at the beginning of the book (page xxii); the suggestions apply equally to all the themes and will show you what to do step-by-step.
- If you are curious to learn more, take a look at the What if I want to do more? section at the back (page 188) for resources to help you on your way.
- Get started!

Be Bloody Good

Overview

We are what we repeatedly do. Excellence, then, is not an act, but a habit.

Aristotle

The Inner Game is about building the foundation of your career to reflect what's inside you. Be Bloody Good explains the next theme: people who thrive are Bloody Good at what they do. This section explores what Bloody Good looks like and what Tarzans and Janes bring to the table. It shows you how to put together your personal profile of success and encourages you to distinguish yourself by knowing your strengths, polishing and honing them in creative ways. Discipline and rigour can be energising, helping you reap the greatest rewards in making a strong and positive contribution.

It takes a closer look at how to build strong, authentic working relationships, particularly when working with the opposite sex, moving away from 'he and she' and towards 'me and we', and invites you to check how you need to flex your own style to get the right results.

And what's up for grabs is a sense of confidence in how much you have to offer, satisfying working relationships and a substantial reputation.

These three steps provide the backdrop against which you can create your unique value proposition:

1   What's my profile?
2   Emotional intelligence and empathy
3   He, she, me, we

Step 1: What's my profile?

What's in it for me?

With a firm grasp of what makes up a stand-out perform-ance, you can begin to identify your unique combination of strengths and formulate your plans to master your craft and make your mark as you bumblebee your way to achieving your frog goals.

The good news

Change is possible and highly achievable if you are moti-vated and dedicated. But before setting off on the wrong path, remember this: you don't have to be good at everything to excel. Would it have lessened his genius if Shakespeare had been a poor decision-maker? Managing around weaknesses, allowing you to hone your strengths, is the name of the game.[1] Focus on what's best in you and be yourself. Benezir Bhutto tells how at the start of her career she felt that as a woman operating in a man's world she had to prove to the men that she had all the male qualities, so she adopted an aggressive style. Her driver was to outdistance and outperform men, until she learned to become comfortable and confident with being herself and played to her own strengths

What's it all about?

The corporate jungle is changing fast and being Bloody Good in today's corporate jungle has moved on apace. What then is cutting edge now? Leaders seeking to build employee engagement prize passion and expertise, together with collaborative, inclusive approaches, in their flatter, leaner, customer-focused companies. This section explores what being Bloody Good looks like according to research and through three role models, and invites you to define your own version.

Here's the first role model.

....

The passionate 'people's banker'

Sarah Deaves, CEO of Coutts, is one of the few women to have risen to such heights in the male-dominated banking world. You might be forgiven for conjuring up the image of a tough, hard-edged, dominating, self-promoting woman. But the reverse would be true. Meeting Sarah you see a friendly, down-to-earth, practical, approachable person. I would even use the word 'ordinary', although she is clearly quite extraordinary, hugely capable, passionate, and focused.

Sarah's international banking career began in marketing. At the university milk round, she remembers meeting a particularly inspiring woman marketer who told her: 'You know you've become completely obsessed with your product when you find yourself discussing the merits of toilet duck, or whatever it happens to be, at a dinner party.' Sarah thought, 'Wow! I can see myself being that passionate and doing that.' Looking around further, she discovered banking and saw what a huge range of career options was possible under one roof – perhaps nothing quite as exotic as toilet duck, but hugely appealing nevertheless.

Her graduate training programme taught her the fundamentals on which she's built her career. A quick learner, she got to understand the mechanics of banking and developed a general knowledge of how things work. So, for example, when she's involved in some re-engineering programme, she knows the processes and issues. She found she had the ability to click into people, to find what they are passionate about, to strike a chord and find common ground so that they are relaxed with her and able to talk naturally. She felt a sense of humility in listening to people talk with pride about their work and watching them put their best into their jobs. These early lessons gave her a powerful foundation in understanding motivation and what energises people and are fundamental to the way she runs her business now.

After the graduate programme, Sarah's next steps appear like a crazy paving path leading her from job to job over the following years. But if you take a closer look, you'll notice an almost perfect career plan, taking her through varied and increasingly complex assignments to equip her for the role of CEO of Coutts: from lending control to setting up specialised services for corporate clients; from strategic planning to marketing a new brand; from an MBA to a remote banking project; from head office roles to local roles; from joint ventures to co-branding partnerships; from legal contracts to takeovers; from international exposure to running a loans bank; from operations and IT to commercial investment.

As well as having Bloody Good knowledge and experience, in Sarah's case, being Bloody Good is made up of the personal competencies and characteristics that are consistent themes and strengths that have made her successful:

- She's extraordinarily open to new experiences and jumps in wholeheartedly, even when she's never done anything like it before.
- She learns quickly, absorbs and assimilates the lessons, fast becoming an expert.
- She has built a strong network right from the beginning. She's made sure she's built her reputation and had the right amount of what she calls 'air cover', so that people

know her and know what she can do. That way, she's always been sought out for new opportunities.

- She's built lasting relationships based on her strong rapport with people. She is good at working as part of a team, getting the best from everyone. Allowing others to develop, too, has meant she's often been able to create her successor before moving on.

- She's straightforward and delivers on her promises to people, building strong trust.

- She thrives on difficult situations and turmoil. She's good at getting in and calming things down. She likes to burrow in and understand how things work.

- She loves her work, works with great people and has huge fun.

What being Bloody Good looks like will look different depending on your sector, your company, your speciality and your role. Here is a list of what is prized by organisations, based on a recent piece of research.[2] Notice how many of Sarah's strengths appear.

While reading through, check out how you stack up and rate yourself.

Table 2 ● How do you stack up?

Example format: Strong? OK? Room for improvement?

Strength	How do I stack up?
Adaptability: having a mindset that embraces change and the ability to learn from experience and adjust accordingly	
Analytical ability: the ability to navigate through complex data	

Strength	How do I stack up?
Authenticity: building trust and having integrity; being open and honest. It also means being consistent and keeping your word	
Coaching: the ability to develop others, bringing out the best in them through a balance of self-discovery and specific feedback	
Communication: the ability to engage and influence others; to have impact, expressing yourself well, verbally, non-verbally and in writing	
Customer focus: having a mindset that puts customers at the heart of everything you do	
Decision-making: the ability to weigh things up quickly, particularly where there is uncertainty and ambiguity	
Drive and passion for results: having a mindset of achievement and enthusiasm for what you're doing	
Emotional Intelligence: the ability to understand yourself and understand others; being self-confident and in control of your emotions	
High standards and rigour: having a mindset that demands the highest quality; going over and above what is expected	

Strength	How do I stack up?
Learning agility: the ability to learn from mistakes and pick new things up quickly	
Managing diversity: having a mindset of willingness to understand difference and embrace it	
Managing time: the ability to plan and organise your workload; meeting deadlines balanced with managing stress levels	
Networking: the ability to build strategic working relationships in and outside the organisation	
Strategic thinking: the ability to see the big picture, especially around global competition and the application of technology	
Team focus: having the mindset that puts team and company results before your own; it's about supporting others and being collegiate	
Receptive to feedback: having a mindset that welcomes, accepts and acts on constructive feedback	

Prioritise these in descending order with your highest strengths first and we'll return to them in the How do I stack up? section (page 72).

Tarzan and Jane and strengths

There are patterns of differences in what Tarzan and Jane bring to the table. Generally speaking, Janes naturally have high levels of emotional intelligence, strong empathy and service industry know-how that the modern economy needs. They are praised and admired for their different and innovative ways of thinking, their ability to build relationships and empower others, their higher academic achievements and greater productivity. Tarzans are seen as better at decision-making and more risk oriented, good at creating the game plan without getting stuck in the mire. They generally outscore Janes on self-confidence, financial acumen, global perspective and industry knowledge, and are better at self-promotion. A combination of both styles in teams and on boards will generate a better modus operandi and sounder solutions: focused, yet willing to explore options; decisive, yet able to consider wider implications; consultative, yet willing to take action.

Consider Deb Covey's career in the light of her unique combination of strengths.

....

The woman who moves mountains of people to do massive things – II

Leading 10,000 people and overseeing a capital budget of around £1.3 billion, Deb Covey is clearly accomplishment oriented. Her trademark speciality is taking complex organisations and sorting them out, making them efficient and getting people to enjoy what they do. As far as she's concerned, people transformation is the key factor that has allowed her to do what she's done and be where she is. She has the ability to see the many parts of a strategy, how they all fit together and intertwine. 'I love the machinery of progress. I set about creating the business plan – a well-balanced architecture that balances financial objectives with meeting the customers' expectations – then I translate it into what it means for people.'

She always expects near impossible goals from her teams, and they don't always engage with her huge demands. Deb will show them the big picture, the magnetic north, and then she'll break down the enormous task into incremental steps: step one, step two, step two-and-a-half. And she insists that they celebrate success along the way, after each step has been achieved. With each incremental step the confidence and momentum increase.

That is how she's got to where she is. Though this says more about her method, it really is how she's got there. Every job since 1979 has been approached in more or less the same way, each getting progressively larger, with more and more responsibility. She's not technical, nor is she an engineer; her job is to manage really, really, really bright engineers. She lets them know that she is not there to tell them how to design, that's their job. But she is there to tell them how to be more productive, how to accomplish the company's goals and how to bring people along with them to do that. She pays attention; she watches people to uncover what makes them tick: 'That way, I can move mountains of people to do massive things. I'm what in the USA you'd call a turnaround agent. I don't like to run a smooth, established business. I like getting started from first base.'

She's a multi-tasker who gets bored doing one thing at a time and has always overtasked herself in projects. Her ultra-complex job is bigger than anything she's ever done. She describes her approach as opening the toolbox she's built over 25 years to find the right tool to use at the right time.

'How cool is that! It doesn't get much better than that, does it? I would never trade this.'

....

Her signature strengths, strong visionary leadership and people transformation have made the hugely complex achievable, enabling Deb to achieve what she has, knowing what to opt in and out of. The same is true for you.

How do I stack up?

Here are two feel-good tasks that people love doing at my seminars.

1 Throughout your life you will have done things that gave you a great sense of pride and satisfaction even though they may now seem quite small and trivial. Some may have been connected with work and many of them may have been to do with hobbies, home and family. It's good to start with childhood examples, as we're hard-wired pretty early on. I remember one woman on a seminar sharing her example. A childhood achievement she was proud of was mastering the game of 'jacks', in which spiky metal pieces are thrown and then picked up between bounces of a small ball. She had arrived at a new school mid-term, when all the other children were already settled. The playground game was jacks, which she'd never played before. So she bought a set and practised and practised and practised at home. And then practised some more. Everywhere: in the kitchen, in the hallway, in her bedroom and in the garden. At any time: before breakfast, after dinner and all other times in between. Until, finally, she became brilliant at it and played to win with all the others.

What themes emerge? Her drive to achieve, her sheer persistence, her competitiveness, her need to belong, all of which manifested themselves as key drivers for her success as an adult.

Take a cashmere-socks moment and reflect on the patterns of achievements that emerge from memorable successes throughout your life.

● Make a list of around ten of your most significant achievements – things you feel you did well, that you enjoyed doing and that you're proud of. They can be as small as a game of jacks or as big as your marriage. Start from childhood, work up to the present and don't bother with modesty.

● For each, jot down specifically what happened and what you did to make it happen, why it was a success and how you felt.

What themes and strengths are emerging?

2 Here's another approach to building up a picture of your strengths:[3]

● Make a list of things that you really enjoy at work. Generally, we are good at what we like, for example listening to people.

● Translate these into key strengths you bring to your workplace; for example, 'my ability to listen effectively enables me to gather data from reluctant sources'.

● Consider how these distinguish you from others; for example, ability to gather and report data may be unique in a department where work is mainly to do with producing products.

By now you should have a rich array of things that have made you successful so far, fresh in your mind.

What do I do?

The next step is to build your unique blueprint, your value proposition, made up of your knowledge, your experience, your personal traits and your competencies, also known as skills or behaviours.[4] Start with a blank sheet of paper, draw the four quadrants and start filling them.

Table 3 ● What's my profile?

Knowledge	Experience
Make a list of what you know	*Make a list of what you've done*
School qualifications	Responsibilities you've had
Languages	Projects you've been on
IT skills	Achievements and promotions
Technical knowledge	Different sectors
Degrees	Different roles
Certificates	Different functions
Qualifications	Different countries
Company courses	Have you led teams?
Qualifications gained on activities outside work – are you a closet pianist?	Have you been through a takeover?
	Have you launched a product?
Market knowledge	Have you implemented a system?
Sector knowledge	
Professional knowledge	
Financial knowledge	
Anything else?	Anything else?

Competencies	Personal traits
Make a list of what you're good at	*Describe your personality – who you are*
Look at your 'How do I stack up?' strengths	Ambitious
Look at your themes from the significant achievements exercise	Calm
	Cautious
Ask others for feedback	Creative
Use performance management reports	Driven
	Extrovert
Use assessment data	Intelligent
Use 360-degree data – feedback from a variety of perspectives	Introvert
	Passionate
Use psychometric data – tests that measure ability and aptitude	Self-confident
Anything else?	Anything else?

It's worth mentioning here that in the new corporate jungle, all of us are going to need to embrace technology: although technology has always been seen as the domain of the geeks, this is no longer the case. Increasingly, the way we work, learn and play is now all based on technology.

Mind the gap

What do you do about the gaps? The starting point is your frog goals and stuffed-mushroom values. Knowing what you want and what's important to you will let you know where to focus. Ask yourself what will give you the greatest leverage from energy invested, remembering that making strengths shine more brightly might be better use of your time than ploughing away at a weakness. Your aim should be to achieve a competent level of performance and minimise risks that might result from your weaknesses, but the distinctiveness of your brand will be built on your signature strengths, and that's where your best efforts should be focused. Cashmere-socks and roast-beef thinking are good ways to find creative solutions without limiting yourself.

On the subject of learning, I remember a lecturer once telling a group about his mother, who was 70, and her mother, his grandmother, who was 95. The grandmother was by far the younger woman. Her daughter vegetated in front of the television all day and was stagnating, while the mother kept up to date with the news, was widely read, went to the theatre, talked to people and went to classes to learn new things. Learning keeps us young and alive; it keeps our 'saw sharp', as Stephen Covey puts it when he tells of a man fever-ishly using a blunt saw to fell a tree, too busy sawing to take the time to sharpen his saw and get the job done quickly.[5] It is so disappointing to hear people say: 'You can't teach an old dog new tricks' or 'I know it all, I've been on every course around' or 'I don't have the time to learn new things.' I love it that my 76-year-old uncle is surfing the internet and reading

Table 4 ● Bridging the gaps

Knowledge

What do you need to know to move forward?

For example:

Do an MBA

Go on a finance programme

Get a professional qualification

Learn a new language

Increase your sector and market knowledge

Be known for knowing your stuff and being able to answer 'killer' questions like those of Jack Welch, former CEO of GE (General Electric):

1 What does your global competitive environment look like?

2 In the last three years what have your competitors done?

3 In that same period what have you done?

4 How might competitors attack you in the future?

5 What are your plans to leapfrog them?

(Adapt these to your role and sector)

Experience

What do you need to do to move forward?

For example:

Courageously seize opportunities

Request high-profile projects

Volunteer to give presentations to senior management

Get responsibility and experience working for your favourite charity

Look for your next job and be preparing for it

Lead a team

Change function

Get strategic experience

Take an assignment abroad

Get a mentor

Partner with someone strong in a complementary area

Network inside and outside the organisation

Competencies

Get on a training programme

Go on a sales training course – good for influencing and relationship building

Get a mentor

Get a coach

Partner with someone strong in a complementary area

Join an acting class (for loads of creativity and to hone your performance skills)

Read books; talk to people; use the internet

E-learning

Observe role models

Keep asking for feedback and measuring improvement

Use the nearest HR adviser and tap into the organisation's resources

Practise! Practise! Practise!

Personal traits

It's perfect to be who you are. Most traits have strong upsides: they are likely to be serving you well in some way. Only work on things that are holding you back or causing you pain.

Get a personal coach

Go on a Neuro-Linguistic Programming (NLP) course – great insights and shifts

Declare to your team what you're working to change – put your money where your mouth is

Get trusted people to act as your 'mirror' and remind you when you're off track blogs to keep up to date; I love it that my 85-year-old mother is helping in a class for adult literacy and learning the piano. 'Constant development,' as Gandhi teaches us, 'is the law of life.'

The Pareto principle, or the 80:20 rule, says that 80% of success comes from 20% of effort. To be most effective:

- focus on the result, not the effort
- look at your exceptional results and identify what you did to achieve them
- be excellent at a few things rather than average at many
- identify your core capabilities and develop these.

With this in mind, now is an opportunity to reflect on your own learning. Repeat the previous exercise by filling in the four quadrants, this time looking at how to bridge the gaps.

I recommend that you combine the two tables, adding the gap-filling activities in Table 4 (page 76) to the strengths in Table 3 (page 74).

Table 5 ● Combination: sample format

Knowledge	Experience
Strengths	Strengths
What I want to enhance	What I want to enhance
What I plan to do, specifically	What I plan to do, specifically
Competencies	**Personal traits**
Strengths	Strengths
What I want to enhance	What I want to enhance/check
What I plan to do, specifically	What I plan to do, specifically

This then becomes a live, working document for you and will be well thumbed and scribbled on as you integrate it into your brand. (There's a spare copy for you to use in the Appendix – see page 208.) There's a fringe benefit too: it will keep your confidence levels high as you keep in mind how good you are. Being Bloody Good is an evolving state. Having rigorous development plans and applying them with energy and enthusiasm will keep your learning alive and your saw sharp. Here's the third example of someone who is Bloody Good. She's worked hard to master her craft.

....

The sensible Sally

Rukhsana Pervez is the youngest regional manager to sit on the management team in the part of Chevron she serves. She zaps all over the world, manages a team of six and is still only 31. 'I'm very boring and ordinary,' she claims. She calls this being a 'sensible Sally'. So how did a sensible Sally get to be so successful?

The middle child of Pakistani-born parents, she was raised with a strong parental message about the importance of education as a strong foundation for anything she wanted to do: go to school, do well; go to university, do well; get a job, do well. She was always thinking about her next steps, always had a plan, always determined and always wanting more. 'I'm the sort of person who runs towards responsibility,' she explains. 'I like to be one step ahead of the game.' So much so that she had already secured her first job before starting her final year at university without setting foot near a university milk round. Hugely driven to be Bloody Good, one of her core mantras is 'actions speak louder than words'. She's able to quickly diagnose what's going on in a situation and then cut to the chase while others are still navel gazing. 'So what?' she'll ask. 'What are we going to do about it?' And she has the persistence to see things through and make sure that things happen.

As it happens, the results she has achieved to date have been a combination of planning mixed with a healthy measure of things not working out. When her plans fail, new doors have invariably opened, and Chevron has been a great place for support and new opportunities. She lives by what she calls her 'three big rules of life', which have always guided her well and are now instinctive: her parents, her religion and her ambition. Within these headings sit key strengths: authenticity, communication, drive and passion for results, emotional intelligence, high standards and rigour, the ability to build trust. These make up her brand of professionalism. Her biggest mistakes have come when she didn't follow her instinct and her rules about what's right.

She feels she at last has a solid base; she has credibility and experience; and she is Bloody Good at what she does, earned through her bloody hard work.

Rukhsana has dedicated all her achievements to her father, who died suddenly when she was 21. She'll often think to herself, 'Dad, did you see what I just did?'

....

Conclusion

By now you're really clear about your strengths and the unique contribution you make; you have creative ideas and plans that will increase your performance, making sure that you're Bloody Good and playing at the top of your game. The next two steps focus on two particularly important strengths worthy of attention: emotional intelligence and empathy; and how to adjust your communication to fit both Tarzans and Janes.

Step 2: Emotional intelligence and empathy

What's in it for me?

Developing your skills of empathy will have a positive impact on your relationships with clients, colleagues, bosses and employees. It will help you to get buy-in to your ideas, which in turn will have a positive impact on your ability to influence, negotiate and win people over. CEOs tell me that qualifications for the job are a 'given'; it is emotional intelligence skills, including empathy, that are the big differentiator and an important ingredient found in high performers. Daniel

Goleman's research shows that emotional intelligence competencies as a whole account for 85% of what sets outstanding apart from the average.[6]

The good news

Having empathy, understanding others, may not come naturally, whether you're a Tarzan or a Jane, but it is a learnable skill and it will work for you immediately and every time. That doesn't mean getting your own way or winning every time, but it does mean building good relationships and getting the most out of each situation every time.

What's it all about?

I remember once struggling with the process of upgrading my mobile phone when everything that could possibly go wrong did go wrong. I was passed from one person to another in the company as I tried in vain to resolve my problem. Every time someone said 'I can't help you in this department' or 'sales should have dealt with this for you' or 'you've got it wrong, madam, we never do that,' my frustration and stress levels went through the roof as my humour and politeness flew out the window. It only needed one person to 'get it', to understand how I was feeling, own the problem and take action for me to capitulate completely, become charm personified and sing their praises ever after. We all have a hugely strong need to be understood. Most of us think we're right anyway so it's only logical that we expect others to see things our way. That's what sits at the heart of this section.

As organisations have a greater need to retain talent and be closer to the customer, there is an increasing need for people with high levels of emotional intelligence and empathy. Twenty years ago it was sufficient to build brand trust through quality and consistency; today brand trust is earned through the emotional relationship between the brand and the consumer. The world of Tarzans is more about intelligence quotient (IQ) than emotional intelligence quotient (EQ), whereas Janes are typically more collaborative and empathetic, and better at building relationships – key components of EQ.

Emotional intelligence hit the corporate headlines when Daniel Goleman, the guru of the subject, published his book of the same name in 1995. EQ is about our capacity for recognising our own feelings and those of others, for motivating ourselves and for managing emotions effectively in others and ourselves. Generally speaking, there are two components: the first comprises self-awareness, self-regulation and self-confidence, all part of the Inner Game. This section explores the second component, the outer part, used in managing relationships. It's about reading and understanding people and being able to see things from a different perspective; in other words, it's about empathy. A dictionary definition of empathy is 'the power of understanding and imaginatively entering into another person's feelings'. It's about being able to shift our perspective on things, to understand others by seeing the world through their eyes, or to stand in their shoes. This is not the same as sympathy, which is about sharing the emotions of another person; understanding is not the same as 'I feel the same'. So it wouldn't have helped me if the customer services manager at the mobile phone company had said, 'Oh, I feel so angry too, madam.'

Why then is empathy viewed by some as negative? Probably because people wrongly think of it as having to show concern, having to be nice to people. We've all witnessed the personality transplants of people fresh from a communications skills course, oozing a false niceness that is quite alien to their usual style. Empathy, like everything else, is about being yourself, being straight and authentic, acting in a way that is consistent with your personality. It's not something you do once, get the formula right and that's that. It's an organic skill that means fine-tuning your responses and approaches and making adjustments; you may get things wrong, but you can always go back and put things right.

For leaders reading this book, here's a salutary statistic: the number one reason that people leave organisations is because of a poor relationship with their boss.[7] Bosses, both Tarzans and Janes, need to hone their relationship-building skills, Albert Ellis believes.

....

The evolved accountant

Albert Ellis thought he'd be a musician. But he didn't cut the mustard and so retired early at the age of 21 after only four years in the industry. He became an accountant instead. And using his profession as his platform, he has thrived. His brand is all about passion, decency, pace, energy and clarity. He never had any overwhelming aspirations for the top job, nor was he ambitious for status or cash per se, but he unconsciously always looked and acted like the next role up, and promotions came without him looking for them. His ability to put himself in his bosses' shoes, to understand their agenda, to align his interests with theirs, has been a mental preparation for their role. He has ended up quite naturally as CEO at Harvey Nash.

The first priority of the CEO of a large organisation is to surround himself with extraordinarily capable and talented business specialists who execute. The obvious solution is to hire from the outside. Albert has done this many times but he is most passionate about his approach to develop and promote 'inside' talent. He believes you need emotional intelligence, intellect and ambition to succeed and has worked hard at unleashing the potential in his teams. He encourages the leaders to look after their people. 'If you look after your people, I will look after you.' In his experience, those who have focused purely on themselves have always failed. 'Being a humble servant leader is what makes you valuable.'

For a Tarzan CEO in what is often perceived as a hard-edged industry, Albert is unusually open and honest. He is open to feedback and, with his executive coach, actively works on his own self-development. For someone in his position, in his sector, he is also, refreshingly, quite a Jane; you'd probably rate him as being emotionally intelligent. His self-awareness is part of it, but what I also see is a high level of empathy. He has learned to put himself in others' shoes. Not doing so has led to harsh mistakes and he has paid the price in some relationships. 'We always think we're right and we see the world a certain way. This can limit our flexibility and effectiveness.'

....

Lack of emotional intelligence generally, and the empathy part of it specifically, wastes time, erodes productivity and increases hurt and frustration; it closes people down and diminishes them in some way.

Sarah Deaves, CEO of Coutts, describes the effect of a difficult boss early on in her career. 'The worst boss I ever had was a woman who'd take credit for others' ideas and had a way of undermining people.' Her style sapped energy and confidence, leaving people in the team feeling debilitated, upset and too preoccupied to be productive. This experience taught Sarah a valuable lesson: never be that kind of boss yourself because you get far more from people when you are emotionally aware.

This section is also about developing the ability to see things from a different perspective. This will help diminish the natural tendency to jump to conclusions and increase the options we have to make better decisions.

Maybe you remember a fantastic advertisement for one of the broadsheet newspapers a few years ago. An old woman shuffled her way slowly down the road, her pension money just visible in her shabby handbag. We watched with a rising feeling of fear and disgust as a thuggish young man wearing a hooded sweater ran towards her. We correctly anticipated the inevitable as he caught up with her and pushed her violently to the ground. We felt so angry and upset at the cruelty and injustice, so critical of the man and the society that had led to his behaviour. It left a bitter taste in our mouths. The camera then panned out, showing the scene from a different perspective. We could see a huge crate falling from a crane above the old woman, so the young man had been rushing to rescue her and in pushing her to the ground had saved her life.

How often does this happen in reality? Without waiting to see the full picture, we develop a distorted picture of reality, based on incomplete information.

We each have a unique way of perceiving the world based on our experiences, memories, beliefs, values and the culture that we grew up in. Our 'map' of the world is as unique as a fingerprint and there are as many maps as there are people. They are all different. Yet we operate as if we are right; that's the way things are. We jump to conclusions, make judgements, have opinions and feel things based on this certain knowledge. We just know that young thugs in hooded jumpers are up to no good. But there is always a different perspective that will show that a different truth is possible. The greater our ability to pan out from a situation and to see it differently, the greater our ability to understand others and the greater our flexibility in selecting options.

This section invites you to expand your perspective, to build up your emotional intelligence by increasing your levels of empathy through a deeper understanding of others, and offers practical ways to do this.

How do I stack up?

My guess is that you're probably pretty aware of your emotional intelligence and your empathy levels already, and of how much your own agenda gets in the way of effective relationships. Here are a few questions to reflect on and to help you to clarify still further.[8] Answer 'often', 'sometimes', 'rarely', 'never':

- Can you tell when your own emotions are getting in the way?
- Do you recognise when your thoughts are becoming negative?
- How often do you stop and think before jumping to conclusions?
- Do you actively seek ways of resolving conflict?
- Are you able to influence others about the way things are done?
- Do others trust and confide in you?
- Are you able to raise morale and make others feel good?
- How often do you offer help and support to others?
- Do you disclose appropriate personal information to build trust with others?
- Do you make a point of involving others in making decisions or finding solutions?
- How often do you praise or recognise others?
- How often do you give constructive feedback?
- Are you able to understand how others are feeling?
- Are you good at really listening to others?
- Do you speak openly about issues or concerns you have at the time they occur?

It's a crude indicator, but the more you scored 'often', the higher your EQ and empathy levels are likely to be. Another way to find out is to be brave and ask someone else to answer the same questions about you and then compare the ratings. By the way, asking for feedback is an emotionally intelligent thing to do; it shows you're building self-awareness and helps to build trust.

What do I do?

1 Back to basics

There are some simple steps to weave into your approach when communicating with people. First, a reality check.

Take a blank sheet of paper and jot down the thoughts that come into your mind when thinking about people who are effective at building relationships.

- What do you think are the best ways to engage people and get their buy-in?
- What gets your buy-in?
- What reduces your level of engagement?
- Who are good role models?
- What specifically do they do to build that relationship?
- Who are bad role models?
- What have they done or not done, said or not said that make them ineffective?

Prioritise so that you have your top five or six.

Here is a list of the answers people generally come up with when asked the questions above. Check them against yours. Do you agree?

- Show respect for me; tell me what's going on; give me positive and constructive feedback.
- Listen to what I have to say, don't talk at me. Ask questions and don't make assumptions.
- Be supportive; understand the issues I'm dealing with and understand what I need.
- Get my ideas and don't just tell me what to do.
- Be open and honest, have integrity and share your views and concerns with me.
- Be organised; prepare for our meetings; agree what needs to be covered and show up.
- Follow through and do what you say you will do.

Add or subtract until you come up with a list that makes most sense to you. Remembering not to have a personality transplant, following these simple basics will have an enormous impact on the effectiveness of your communication with others. Until they become a habit, prepare in advance. Add to your preparation checklist from the Inner Game (and there's a spare copy in the Appendix on page 204). For example:

- What feedback will I give?
- How will I show respect for this person?
- What questions will I ask?
- What support might they need from me?
- What is appropriate for me to share?

2   *Active listening*

The word for listen in Chinese incorporates listening with the whole of you: ears, eyes, heart and undivided attention.

Turning the volume down on our self-talk is about tuning into what others are saying and what they're not saying; it's about noticing what they're saying with their body language as well as with their words. Focusing on others is like displacing more murky water in the bucket with another pebble: the more we concentrate on them, the more we really listen, and the more options we have. Research by TACK International showed that buyers rated good questioning and real listening skills as the most valued of a salesperson's contribution.[9] A CEO I worked with had strong views and ingrained ideas

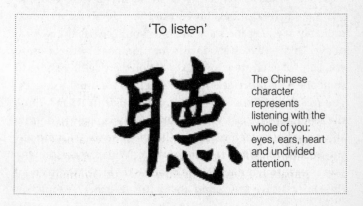

'To listen'

The Chinese character represents listening with the whole of you: eyes, ears, heart and undivided attention.

and was pretty keen to share his pearls of wisdom in board meetings. He was so vocal that others learned to be quiet and not say what they thought at meetings. The real work would be done after he'd left. He came to see that although he had hired smart people, he wasn't using them. At one meeting he tried something different. He made a point of asking everyone round the table what they thought before he offered his opinion. What he learned was that every one of his ideas came up but, more importantly, more and better ones came up too. He learned to shut up and trust his people.

Another way of really listening is to tune into the language people are using and respond in a way that will have the most impact. Generally, people process information in four key ways:

● through images
● through sounds
● through feelings and bodily sensations
● through analysis.

We all have a preferred system, but we are likely to use more than one. If you spend time with me, you soon get to know that I prefer things presented visually, and my conversation is likely to be peppered with words that reflect this: look, see, visualise, reflect, view, show. If you were going to sell me a pair of shoes, how would you go about it? You'd probably say: 'Let me *show* them to you. *Look* at the *rich red colour*. They will *look* good with your jumper. Try them on so you can *see* what they look like.' If you were selling shoes to someone who processes through feelings, you might say: 'Do you *feel* good in them? Are you *comfortable* in them? *Touch* the suede -- it's so *soft*.' With the analytical person you'd probably talk about practical things: the *price*, the *value* for money, the *workmanship*, *how* to care for them. With the person who processes through sounds, you'd talk to them, tell them about the shoes: 'Have you *heard* about this designer? People *say* these are best for the feet. I can almost *hear* the compliments you'll get. I love the *sound* they make on the floor.' We may want information from more than one system, so mix your words; I'm likely to be interested in comfort and cost, as well as the look of the shoes.

See if you can find (visual) the many ways to tune into (sound) what systems people are using (analytical) so you can sense (feeling) which are the best words to use when communicating with them. The benefits of listening out for language are:

- you'll be actively listening to them
- you'll understand something more about them
- you'll get a better response if you use their preferred system.

If you want to know what your preferred representational systems are, take two minutes to write about something you enjoy or record yourself talking about something you enjoy. Go back and listen or read and analyse the kinds of words you've used. That's your best clue. There are also online representational systems questionnaires, easy to find with an internet search.

3 Look at things from a different perspective

Albert Ellis, CEO of Harvey Nash, has learned to think outside his own box by asking himself what it is like in the other person's head, by asking 'how are my words and actions being perceived?'.

He tells of a time when one of the senior managers in his team was displaying erratic, aggressive behaviour and having a negative impact on those around him. He was on a path of self-destruction and it was causing a major problem. A typical response would have been to take the corporate line and question his role in the company. But, driven by the desire not to lose him, Albert looked at the situation anew. He forced himself to take on the role of the other individual, really getting inside his head and seeing the world through his eyes. Doing this made him see with blinding clarity that through his own actions he had inadvertently trampled over all that the person held dear. He realised that bruised self-esteem was behind the erratic aggression. In this way, Albert was able to unlock the problem and take decisive action. He apologised. He took responsibility. And he promoted the man. This was completely 'left field', the exact opposite of what people expected and what Albert had originally felt like doing, but it restored trust and he believes it was the quickest fix he's ever made. The manager turned the corner and went on to thrive. Albert often uses this technique to find answers where they are not obvious and where he needs that extra degree of empathy.

Bearing in mind that there is no 'right' perspective, accessing other perspectives will unlock our thinking and provide opportunities for 'left field' insights and creative options. The technique that Albert describes is one of my absolute favourites. You don't need to talk or write, just experience it. Here's what to do:

- Identify the relationship.
- Stand or sit as if you are with the person. What is your view of the situation? What are you feeling? How are you behaving? What are you seeing in the other person? What are your beliefs? What's wrong?
- Now switch positions so that you are standing or sitting in the other person's place looking at yourself. Make an imaginative leap to understand the world from their perspective. Take on their body language, posture and breathing. Take on their values and beliefs. What's it like in their head and what's it like in their body? As that person: what is your view of the situation? What are you feeling? How are you behaving? What are you seeing in

the other person (you)? What are your beliefs? What's wrong? What do you need? How best can the other person help you?

● Now switch positions again so you are sitting away from the first two positions. This time take on the role of an outsider, someone detached from the situation, who can see the relationship between the two viewpoints. How are they each behaving? What do they each believe? What is there to be learned? What advice do you have for the first person (you)? What does that person need to do?

● Now return to your own chair bringing your new learning and perceptions with you. How has your perception changed? What's different? What have you learned?

You can use this exercise to build your empathy levels when preparing for a meeting, a presentation, a client pitch, a problem discussion, an interview – anywhere it would be useful to understand another person's position. If there is more than one person, take a different chair for each and repeat the process. Ideally, do this with a partner or a coach who can pose the questions, leaving you free to get under the skin of each person, remembering that you don't need to say a word, just experience it. You can do it on your own, but it takes more concentration.

I was once on a course that was fast-paced and full of difficult, highly complex concepts. As I was struggling to grasp the most basic information, I noticed a particularly bright woman who had clearly not only grasped, but had also absorbed and was using all the new concepts with ease. Mulling this over next morning in bed (another great place for cashmere-socks thinking), I decided to try this technique to see whether I could understand more about her learning process. I made an imaginative leap to experience the world from her perspective and what it was like in her head. In doing so, I got an extraordinary sensation of a light flashing on and off at high speed in my head, almost as if a camera were clicking away. It was non-stop and exhausting; I was glad to stop. When I told her about this next time we met, she confirmed that she had a photographic memory, absorbing and remembering things very quickly by taking mental pictures. From that exercise, I learned that there was a choice: I could practise and develop the skill of taking mental pictures or I could choose a different way to process information. I came to feel comfortable about my own slower, non-visual learning process, thinking the new ideas through and finding relevant applications for them so that they make sense to me and get remembered.

4 *As if*

If it's true that we behave in accordance with our beliefs, it follows that if we change our beliefs we may change our behaviour. In the context of empathy, here's a different 'as if' exercise to flex your thinking.

Put on your cashmere socks and select one of the beliefs below. You don't have to believe it to be true, but if you try it on 'as if' it were true, reflect on what is different:

- Everyone has a unique map of the world.
- Everyone is doing the best they can with the resources they have.
- All behaviour has a positive intention.
- The meaning of communication is the response that you get.
- The person with the most flexibility of behaviour has the greatest influence on others.
- Everyone is in charge of their mind and therefore their results.

If you don't quite get one of them, guess at what you think it might mean and use that, or move on to another. This is a good one to do in your hippy group. Each person takes on a different belief and spends one day acting as if it were true, and then reports back on what they've learned.

Conclusion

Focusing on other people, understanding where they are coming from, is what empathy is about. Add to that the Inner Game aspects of self-awareness, self-regulation and self-confidence and you have a pretty good understanding of emotional intelligence. It is an important strength, highly valued in the new corporate jungle and typically one that Tarzans need to polish up.

The next step is for Tarzans and Janes to be Bloody Good at communicating with each other.

Step 3: He, she, me, we

What's in it for me?

Being Bloody Good at relating to any different culture, but specifically gender culture, will give you huge flexibility in building positive, effective relationships. This will have an impact on the buy-in you get and how well you influence others in all contexts. Your message will be received loud and clear, and not lost in the cacophony of clashing planets.

The good news

Dame Edith Evans once said, 'When a woman behaves like a man, why doesn't she behave like a nice man?' She makes a good point and it's also true in reverse. We certainly don't have to take on the worst traits of the other gender in order to be accepted by them. We don't have to be anything other than authentic. We're only talking about flexing our style to meet others in their world.

What's it all about?

As one of the trailblazing female leaders in the notoriously Tarzan-led telecoms industry, Deb Covey, of BT, was the only woman at management meetings in the early days of her career. One event is etched indelibly on her memory. In 1993 she was invited to a conference held in a country club. As she drove up to the security hut at the end of the drive, they thought she was there to join the kitchen staff, as, she discovered, it was a male-only club. She explained that she was there in her own right as a manager attending the conference. But there was no way round the club's protocol and she was asked if she'd mind coming in through the kitchen, as they couldn't possibly let her through the main entrance. 'Yes I would,' she asserted. She called her boss and insisted that he come and get her. 'Why did you select a venue where no woman was allowed in?' she demanded. It had simply not occurred to him to think about Deb but it certainly never happened again.

The corporate jungle is changing. Stories like Deb's and the old rules of engagement are slowly disappearing. Women now make up nearly half the workforce, with more and more of them leapfrogging into management and beyond. Juan Villalonga, former chairman of Spain's Telefonica, goes as far as saying: 'I believe that women's advancement is virtually unstoppable. Women will be the ones running the world in 100 years' time.'[10] This means many variations on a theme: Tarzans will be leading upwardly mobile, Bloody Good Janes; more and more Tarzans will be reporting to Jane bosses; Janes will be stepping outside the safe circle of the sisterhood and leading other women. A new generation of Janes is steadily taking control of the nation's purse strings and it's only a matter of time before their assets outstrip men's.

Many of my clients are male private bankers who tell me that they are a bit stuck when it comes to building comfortable working relationships with women. They identify a need to upgrade their approach and acquire some new skills as so many of their clients are now wealthy and powerful women. A female CEO told me about her experience with a male banker when seeking to set up a new business account. He was apparently a bit of a dinosaur from the old school of banking, 'male, pale and stale'. An initial meeting to discuss banking needs was set up. Her husband just happened to be with her because they were going out afterwards, so the banker added two and two together and came up with the wrong answer. He made some incorrect assumptions and addressed his entire conversation to the husband, overlooking the CEO completely. 'In London to do some shopping?' was his only comment to her. Needless to say, he didn't get her business. This need for new relationship-building skills extends to powerful female clients in other areas, too.

We've seen that with different values in play, new Tarzans are beginning to want different things and cries of 'quality of life' are beginning to echo around the boardrooms. They want to take their kids to school; they want to leave their BlackBerries at home when they're on holiday. And they're used to women working; many of them have partners, sisters and mothers who are career Janes. We've also seen that ambitious Tarzans and Janes build their confidence, take responsibility for their own careers and just get on with it.

Rukhsana Pervez of Chevron began her career in the motor industry and moved from there to the oil industry, both well known as Tarzan-dominated industries. Being both young and female, initially she was not taken seriously. This did not put her off; in fact she decided to ignore it. She had confidence in herself, knowing her strengths and knowing clearly 'I can do this'. Her take on the glass ceiling is that it's just old baggage and traditional insecurity. Now for so many people it simply isn't there. For her part, she hasn't let it bother her and does not see it as a big deal; she just gets on with it.

To be Bloody Good, we too need to navigate around the issues and get on with it. This section highlights the cultural differences between us (he and she) so that we can adapt our language and flex our style to reduce misunderstandings between Tarzans and Janes to build enjoyable, productive and creative working relationships (me and we). It is important to remember that this is not about putting down one style or another because neither is right or wrong; neither is good or bad. We need to respect and embrace both styles to thrive, while remaining authentic and true to ourselves. Remembering that men can be Janes and women can be Tarzans, it is also important to recognise that men and women may have parts of both in them. When we work with people from a different country, we already make sure that we prepare thoroughly, taking responsibility for learning about their culture, customs and values. Now it's time to do the same with gender culture.

Different planets

Remember the old joke: 'How many men does it take to change a toilet roll? No one knows. It's never been done.' And the other one I like: 'Why does it take three women with PMT to change a light bulb? BECAUSE IT JUST DOES.'

There are plenty more where those came from; I'm sure you have your own particular favourites. Beyond the jokes there is an array of cards, fridge magnets, chain e-mails and books, all attesting to the fact that men and women are just different, creatures from altogether different planets. Tarzans and Janes have different cultures and different rules of engagement and we're all increasingly aware of them. In everyday conversation it's not uncommon now to hear Tarzans confirm, 'we all know that I can only do one thing at a time', or Janes say, 'the map-reading gene has passed me by'.

Everyone has stories to tell and views to express on this often amusing, sometimes emotive, subject. At seminars, I get the women together around one flipchart, the men around another, and ask them: 'What are the biggest differences that you notice between the genders?'

At one seminar, before they got started, a participant told everyone of the time that she needed to buy a pair of black shoes to go with a new suit. She persuaded her reluctant husband to go with her and anticipated spending a pleasant afternoon together. They arrived at the shopping centre and went into the first shoe store where she found a suitable style and tried them on. They fitted well and her husband was delighted; job done and time to get back home in time for the Arsenal game.

She, however, was crestfallen. She had been looking forward to a whole afternoon browsing round, looking at all the shoes in all the shops, perhaps stopping for coffee and finally selecting the chosen shoes, which may or may not have been the pair from the first shop. Jane sulks; he obviously doesn't love her. Tarzan hasn't a clue about what he's done wrong. This is a perfect illustration of a clash of cultures. He was focused on the task and solving a problem; she was focused on the process and the relationship. If you change the context of the stereotypical situation from the shopping centre to the boardroom, you start seeing the potential for misunderstandings.

Before I show you what appears on their flipcharts, what's your answer to the question: What are the biggest differences that you notice between the genders? Table 6 provides a summary of typical responses.

Even though these are generalisations, they are based on years of experience of asking this question, and the answers are representative of what I find elsewhere.

Think about the impact of these differences in the world of work. Here's an example. A male leader told me about a high-profile, complex project he wanted to assign to the person in his team most able to deliver a good result. He

Table 6 ● What are the biggest differences that you notice between the genders?

Janes	Tarzans
Multi-task – good at doing more than one thing at a time	Focused – best at doing one job at a time
Tend to have a natural empathy, interested in understanding people and feelings	Tend to concentrate on the work issues and facts
Talk things through when there's a problem	Work things out on their own, internal 'mulling'
Talk to each other and share personal things	Do things together and don't usually talk about personal things
Good at listening and communicating	Good at bargaining and deal brokering
Ask for and offer help	Work it out themselves and let people work things out for themselves
Think out loud; offer lots of options; present the long version of the facts	Get straight to the bottom line
Talk about what they can't do	Talk about what they can do
More ready to accept the blame	Don't take things so personally
More alert to the people factors, sensing changes in employee behaviour	People factors pass the average male manager by
Women can give you a harder time than men	Men can be more forgiving than women
Undersell and over deliver	Oversell and under deliver
Generally conciliatory; not so good at dealing with issues head on	Often aggressive
'Read between the lines' and pick up what is not said	Take communication literally

selected his two best people, a man and a woman. Both were extremely high performers; both were capable of doing the job and neither of them had done anything like it before. He asked them how they would go about the task. The man said, 'I'd do x, y and z.' The woman reflected and said, 'Well I haven't done anything like this before. Hmmm, there are a number of things we could do. We could try a, or possibly b. Or, maybe c would work? What do you think? I'd need to give it some thought.' The man was given the job; the leader preferred his decisive style and found the woman too vague and uncertain. She gave the impression that she doubted her abilities. Actually, this particular Tarzan had no idea whether 'x, y or z' were viable options; they were just ideas, too. And Jane was simply exploring ideas and thinking out loud, interested in the process in keeping with the Jane culture. Neither was wrong or right, they just used different thought processes and communication styles.

When tackling a problem, a man often sorts through all his options internally before offering a solution. To verbalise his thoughts and uncertainty before he has reached a solution could jeopardise his perception in the Tarzan world. Men also tend to have goal-focused minds and want to fix problems or issues as quickly as possible. Women, however, often process issues externally by gathering input from a variety of sources, before reaching a solution. A woman does not think she will lose face by asking for input from outside sources. Goal achievement is just as important to women, but how they get there is different.

David Gold, the entrepreneurial philanthropist and CEO of ProspectUs, finds women in business generally better to deal with, more rounded and open. He wishes those that mimic the male mould wouldn't. His team all assure me that David is much more of a Jane than a Tarzan in his style and approach.

What the researchers say

There is much fascinating research on this subject and it is consistent with what I found out from the people I spoke to. I particularly like the work done by John Gray, *Mars and Venus in the Workplace*,[11] and Pat Heim, *Hardball for Women*.[12] Here's a sample of what researchers are saying so you get a fuller understanding before we move on to what to do with the knowledge.

1 Gender diversity in children

Research shows that the differences between Tarzans and Janes are evident from a very young age. Hilarie Owen, executive director of Renew (Register of Executive and Non-Executive Women), conducted a survey in 2004 to find out what boys and girls from five to eighteen thought of each other.

- The five-year-olds said: 'Boys want to be active and play at war and girls want to talk and include everyone.'

- The nine-year-old boys said: 'Girls can be fussy; they are too kind – they need to be tougher; girls are weak and wimpish; girls are interested in make-up and how they look.'

- The nine-year old girls said: 'Boys think of themselves; they think of war and push their weight around.'

- The eleven-year-olds said: 'Boys are bossy; girls work in teams. Boys are only interested in winning; girls stop and think. Girls are concerned with their appearance and have self-doubt; boys are action oriented. Boys go straight in while girls think of the best way forward.'

The findings from the eleven to eighteen age groups remained consistent:

- Girls said: 'Boys want to start world war three; girls like to play gently. Girls stick at things, girls stop and think; boys just go straight into something. Boys fight; girls try to reason. Girls try to make friends with the group they are leading; boys just get on with it. Girls work as a team; boys tend to take things on by themselves.'

• Boys said: 'Boys like action; girls are more into their appearance. Boys will get in a fight; girls use words. Boys follow one person; girls decide in groups. Boys are more direct; girls think more. Girls are less confident; boys are more competitive.'

In this older group, it wasn't unusual for boys to say they preferred the female way of leadership, but not one girl said she preferred the way boys lead. *Sugar*, a best-selling teen magazine, reinforced the emphasis that young girls put on beauty. They asked teenage girls whether they would prefer to be clever or pretty. The answer was pretty. Teenage boys at the same time were focusing on skills, on being good at things like ball games and computer games.

2 *Relationships*

Games that boys play involve adversarial relationships. Boys learn that competition and conflict are stimulating and fun. They also learn that when the game is over, it's over. According to research conducted by Pat Heim,[13] boys learn early that to win a competition, there must be a leader. This creates a structural hierarchy in which there is always someone above and someone below in status. For the most part, girls play relationship games, like dolls, with one person, a best friend. As a result, girls learn good interpersonal skills and learn how to 'read' others well. An important rule in the female culture is that the power in interpersonal relationships is shared and always kept even. There are no bosses in playing dolls. The girls who tried to be the boss of other girls quickly learned that this behaviour damaged friendships. Consequently, when adult women enter a hierarchical arena they usually attempt to share power equally or flatten the hierarchy. As a result, women often negotiate differences, seeking win-win solutions, focusing on what is fair for all and, above all, harmonious relationships take top priority. One of the hitches for them is that the corporate jungle usually plays by the competitive rules of team sports, where winning is all that matters and aggressive behaviour is perceived as strength. Laura Liswood, Secretary General of the Council of Women World Leaders, observes that women will often want to make sure that the relationship itself doesn't get damaged in the process of the discussion and so will avoid conflict; for men it's more important to be respected than to be liked, so they are usually less concerned about relationships.

In Jane's flat structure, the leadership style at work is involvement. Female managers are more likely to share power with others, involving them in the problem-solving and decision-making process. On the plus side, involvement promotes creativity and gains buy-in when others are included in getting the job done. The downside is that males who are more accustomed to taking orders from above might view them as weak and ineffectual.

3 Communication

In his book *Mars and Venus in the Workplace*,[14] John Gray points out that not only are men and women from different planets, but they speak different languages without realising it: they use the same words but the meanings are different. As a result, men and women make incorrect assumptions about what is being said and fail to understand each other. Misinterpreting a man's choice of words and expressions, a woman sees him as selfish, inconsiderate and less worthy of her trust. Misinterpreting her manner of communicating, a man sees her as incompetent and less worthy of his respect.

For example, women use particular linguistic devices. They:

- hedge their bets with words like 'maybe', 'perhaps', 'I kind of have a problem with this report'
- use disclaimers like 'I may be wrong but…'
- use tag questions which appear at the end of the sentence – 'I think this is the best way to do this, don't you?'

Tarzan is likely to hear, 'I'm not sure what I think.' He prefers more direct language and these devices will make Jane appear indecisive. But these language structures are very functional in the female culture; they flatten the hierarchy and emphasise involvement, both of which are important communication devices used by women when dealing with other women in the work setting. Men use the least number of words to make a point. This kind of communication is limited to facts, figures and logic, with every word used to make a primary point. This can make them appear aggressive and insensitive to Janes, who use words to convey feelings, relieve tension, or discover a point.

4   Verbal and non-verbal conversations

There is also a vast difference between men and women in terms of their sensitivity to non-verbal cues. Men are less likely to see and accurately read facial expressions. Women expect men to be as intuitive as they are and understand what's not being said and to read between the lines; men favour a direct and literal speaking and listening style. There are many non-verbal cues that are misconstrued by men and women at work. Even something as simple as a nod can be misread. Women nod when listening to someone as a way of telling that person, 'I hear what you're saying.' Men, however, nod when they agree.

Deborah Tannen refers to rapport talk versus report talk as she describes the ways men and women engage in conversations:[15]

She: How did things go today?
He: Fine.
She: What did you do?
He: Went to the meeting.
She: What happened at the meeting?
He: Not much.

I have exactly this kind of conversation with my sons, hugely maddening for a Jane and almost intrusive for a Tarzan. Jane tries to establish closeness, it doesn't matter much what they talk about. Tarzan may feel interrogated if she pushes for further information as he feels he has replied to her questions.

5 Meetings

I bought a great card recently showing a classic *Punch* cartoon. It depicts a group of people sitting round a table, five men and one woman. The caption reads: 'That's an excellent suggestion, Miss Triggs. Perhaps one of the men would like to make it.'[16] A particular area of culture clash is meetings: men and women have different ways of perceiving them, as Pat Heim describes. Men usually get all their ducks lined up in a row in advance of a scheduled meeting. For many Tarzans the real meeting happens before the meeting, during breaks in the meeting or after the meeting, but not during the meeting. Women, by contrast, tend to have their meeting during the meeting. When a woman brings up a new subject for the first time at a meeting, she is not trying to 'blind-side' the others, but is simply doing the meeting at the meeting. Men and women do meetings differently. A man who strongly believes in his ideas is likely to speak at length and dominate meetings by discussing those ideas. He generally knows what he wants to say in advance and typically makes statements such as 'obviously, the best way to do this …' and he is more likely to interrupt others. Conversely, a woman will often wait her turn and share the floor. She is also more likely to think out loud, to begin talking and gradually discover what she wants to say, phrasing her ideas, 'don't you think it would be a good idea if ...? As in the *Punch* cartoon, women complain that they are not heard or that their ideas aren't taken seriously.

This brief overview of the leading research highlights just a few of the key areas of difference to raise your awareness of the areas of difference in the two cultures. What counts, though, is what we do with what we know.

How do I stack up?

Take a moment to reflect on the differences outlined in What's it all about? above and simply ask yourself:

- Which of the behaviour patterns am I using?
- Is there a problem? If so, how is it a problem for me?
- What specifically is getting in the way?
- What changes will have the greatest impact?

What do I do?

1 *Awareness*

Sometimes simply being aware is enough to get you doing things differently, almost unconsciously. Just reading through the information and getting a sense of how you communicate, seeing yourself through the eyes of others, will start the process of flexing your style. Here are some ideas to start off with.

While seminar participants are up at their flipcharts, I ask them another question: What are the most important changes you'd like to see the other gender make to communicate better with you? Table 7 summarises the ideas that usually arise.

Table 7 ● What are the most important changes you'd like to see the other gender make to communicate better with you?

Janes	Tarzans
Listen	Be more concise
Use common sense	Don't interrupt
Show more understanding and empathy. Be more aware of the differences between us	Be more decisive
Express your feelings	Be less emotional and don't look for hidden agendas
Talk to us! Be much more communicative	Stick to the point. Be more analytical and focused on the job at hand
Be less aggressive and less confrontational	Don't apologise. Don't say you're not sure about how to approach something
Understand what we're not saying – read between the lines	Be more direct – don't expect us to be mind readers
Be supportive	Don't offer advice
Take an interest in my interests	Let's stick to business
Just listen when we need to let off steam: you don't need to do anything about it	Only complain when you have a solution to suggest

Using and building on these ideas will improve how you're perceived by the other gender and communication will be better. So what can you do? Here are a couple of quick suggestions.

1 For Jane wanting to adapt her style to Tarzan's:

● Prepare for meetings in advance, all meetings; including one-to-one meetings, large meetings, conference calls. This means you can cut out the amount of 'exploring' you need to do and will build your confidence both in standing your ground and making decisions.

● Keep it concise; people don't need every detail. They'll ask if they need to know more. This includes e-mail and voicemail. People will switch off if you're too discursive. A good format for e-mails is to keep them as brief as possible; clarify upfront what the e-mail is about; list the points; summarise the actions, expected outcomes and next steps

2 For Tarzan wanting to adapt his style to Jane's:

● At meetings, ask questions that involve Janes and elicit their ideas. Why would you do this? Guess what, some of their ideas will be better than yours. Taking the time to hear them will produce a better solution.

● Build a relationship, ask how they are; talk to them.

Where else could you adapt your style? What would be most useful for you?

I often hear statements like this from women: 'I feel it is up to me to take on board different personalities, enabling them to focus on my goals in a way that they feel comfortable.' Remembering the lessons of 'poor me', this is absolutely right. The only caveat is that too much responsibility for adapting already sits with women; we know that Janes tend to shoulder the blame for things. Many women's networking or support groups are heavily focused on women changing in order to succeed, but I believe that the responsibility for getting on well should be shared by Tarzans and Janes. That said, taking responsibility instead of complaining about people is the right way to go and is the right frame of mind to foster.

Deb Covey likes to tackle differences head on. She, like other Janes (and other Americans), is non-hierarchical and is comfortable reaching down into the organisation to talk to people. She's discovered, however, that people are terrified of this and assume that they are 'done for' if they are invited to her office. It's unheard of to socialise with people way down the pecking order, even if you get on really well. This is consistent with a Tarzan culture. So Deb has taken personal responsibility for adapting her style, respecting the culture, allowing people to be comfortable. She has learned to be sensitive to the issues and now checks with both men and women: what's the attitude? Are they sensitive to the fact that I'm a Jane?

2 Giving feedback

It's important to adapt your style when giving feedback; not surprisingly, receiving feedback is different depending on whether you're a Tarzan or a Jane. Here are two examples from leaders in very different spheres. Kelly Fordham, a consultant in Rukhsana Pervez's team at Chevron, spent the early part of her career working with the army. She told me about a conversation with a company commander who was experienced in training new officers, both male and female. His view was there was a clear difference in how the young men and women dealt with feedback: 'When I call one of the lads in for a rollicking they will typically listen, absorb it, apologise and walk away – taking it on the chin as it were.' But he had to change his approach with the women, as they would normally question the feedback, wanting to understand all the details before ending the conversation. He noticed that the women would spend far more energy thinking through the feedback and would generally appear to be more concerned about it than the men.

Similarly, Bill Sweetenham, the national British swimming coach, believes that you need to deal with men and women in utterly different ways, understanding what will get the best response. When coaching a woman, he recognises how important it is to build a relationship – knowing when her birthday is, how her family are. He chooses a time when she's in a good mood to give her feedback for improvement. When she's down, he'll make sure that his feedback is positive and encouraging. In general, he will give positive feedback immediately and negative feedback after a couple of days, always focusing on the facts not the person. On the other hand, he finds that when his male coachees are down, they respond to 'a kick'. He can be more direct and less guarded with them.

With these examples in mind, be aware of differences, prepare your approach carefully in advance and tune into the other person before giving your feedback.

3 Rapport

The lessons about empathy apply here too. After all, it's about understanding others' perspectives and putting yourself in their shoes in order to meet them in their world. So, revisit the What do I do? section (page 85) at the end of the empathy step (Step 2), this time thinking about the specific context of Tarzan and Jane: back to basics; active listening; look at things from a different perspective; 'as if'.

There is another concept that applies to enhancing empathy in all contexts: rapport. Building rapport is a natural engagement with another person based on mutual respect. It's more about not doing what gets in the way of rapport rather than artificially creating it. If you sit in a restaurant and watch people, you'll know instantly whether they are getting on or not, whether they're in rapport or not. How do we know this? When people are naturally in rapport with each other, their body language mirrors each other's, like a harmonious dance. As one leans forward so does the other. As one lifts the glass so does the other. As one smiles so does the other. As legs are crossed and unfolded, the other follows. Voice tone matches voice tone; language matches language. This is entirely unconscious and it happens quite naturally and spontaneously. Skills of building rapport include a mindset of openness and respect, listening and interest. It's about being comfortable and authentic.

As you are speaking to Tarzans and Janes, check the levels of rapport:

- Are we comfortable with each other?
- Are we on the same wavelength?
- Are we absorbed and engaged in the conversation?
- Does this feel authentic?
- Am I being myself?

If the answer is 'no', then:

- How can I make them more comfortable with me?
- What is their perception of this conversation?
- What am I putting in the way?
- How can I engage them?

These questions will increase your levels of empathy, understanding and awareness. A word of warning: you cannot build rapport by artificially copying or mimicking another's body language, as some training courses unfortunately teach. To watch a person imitating your gestures and body language is transparent and insulting – the very opposite of rapport. So be natural, be interested and be respectful and you won't go far wrong.

Conclusion

Understanding our differences helps us to move away from divisive 'he and she' towards a more authentic 'me and we'. It shouldn't be a matter of either testosterone or hormones; we can achieve so much more by combining our talents and positively working together. Being aware of the different gender cultures helps us adapt and learn to speak the other's language. This will get us higher levels of trust, respect and buy-in. And it will minimise levels of misunderstanding, hurt and frustration.

Be Bloody Good: conclusion

With a strong Inner Game foundation, the next step is to know just how good you are. We've taken a look at what being Bloody Good looks like for Tarzans and Janes in the 21st century and specifically what that means to you. You've now put your personal profile of success together and thought about how to hone your strengths in creative ways. With finely tuned emotional intelligence and, in particular, empathy, you're now well on your way to communicating powerfully. No longer thinking about 'he and she', you've focused on the 'me' and finally the 'we' to move towards diverse, innovative and authentic working relationships.

What do I do now?

As before, when you went through the exercises and read about the role models, and as you took cashmere-socks moments of reflective thinking, you will have absorbed and integrated some of your insights already so you need take no further conscious action on those.

- Reread the Making it stick section at the beginning of the book (page xxii); the suggestions apply equally to all the themes and will show you what to do step by step.

- If you are curious to learn more, take a look at the What if I want to do more? section at the back (page 188) for resources to help you on your way.

- Get started!

Turn Up The Volume

Overview

In order to be irreplaceable, one must always be different.

Coco Chanel

Imagine yourself as a product on the supermarket shelf. How do you stand out in a crowded market and get picked over others? How do you influence the buying decision? And what's your personal brand?

Who comes to mind when you think of a strong personal brand: maybe Richard Branson? Virgin is one of the world's best-known brands and Branson is completely synonymous with it enabling the brand to stretch to such totally different businesses from records to airlines, from cola to make-up, from trains to mobile phones. Words often associated with Branson's personal brand are: entrepreneur, casual, approachable, challenging, adventurous, fun and service.

People have usually made up their minds about us within four seconds of contact, so the aim is for you to be in charge of the messages you give out, making sure that people 'get' what you're all about straight away, associating you with the things you want to be associated with. Not only that, but you want them to keep 'getting' you consistently.

Turn Up The Volume is not about creating a false impression or trying to be like someone else; it's about being a confident, bolder, crisper, louder and congruent version of you. Turn Up The Volume will show you how to be at the top of people's minds when choices are made. It takes you through the lessons to be learned from branding a product and translates them into creating a personal brand for Tarzans and Janes alike: both have a need and in my experience both have the appetite. It shows you how to fine-tune your own brand and invites you to explore creative ways of communicating it across different senses and across different touch points so that you build a congruent message that is remembered. This theme also takes a good look at how language and non-verbal signals in particular affect perceptions.

And what's up for grabs? Powerful and memorable impact.

The art of personal branding

What's in it for me?

Having your own integrated personal brand message will get you naturally and comfortably to the top of people's minds and you will stand out from the crowd when choices are being made. Being able to answer the question 'what am I best known for?' and to act on it will help you to be distinct.

The good news

Just think of Madonna, constantly reinventing her brand and keeping it fresh and current, evolving from bad girl to material girl to naughty girl: tramp to vamp to earth mother. It's never too late to begin. And the good news is that you're already well on your way because you've begun to define your goals, values and value proposition – what you bring to the party – in the Inner Game and being Bloody Good. It's a relief too to remember that the aim of personal branding is being you, not trying to become like someone else. That would take far too much effort and you could only ever be, at most, a poor second best. For the learned rabbi in folklore, who on his deathbed was asked to account for his life, what was important was not 'Why were you not more like Abraham?' but 'Why were you not true to the best of yourself?'. So this is all about being true to the best in yourself, Turning Up The Volume on your unique style.

What's it all about?

Before we begin, grab a blank piece of paper and have a go at this:

- Think of something that belongs to you, probably an object; something that you absolutely love. Jot it down on your piece of paper.

- Then choose the three adjectives that describe it and convey why you like it so much. List your three words on your page.

For example, I choose my reading glasses; I love glasses. As a child, I always wanted to wear them but had to wait a long time until I needed to. Now at last I do, and I've set about collecting as many funky pairs as I can find. They are all fun, stylish and stand out. Keep your paper handy – we'll return to it soon.

Building a brand is about defining your message, building perceptions and differentiating yourself. Every day, everywhere we go, we are hit by countless brand messages. Our minds are drowned out by the cacophony of each brand fighting to be heard. Each brand must strike the perfect note to stand out. The vital lesson is to develop a totally integrated message, making the most of every signal in such a way that the brand becomes instantly recognisable. According to Shelley Lazarus, chairman and CEO of Ogilvy & Mather Worldwide, a global advertising company, 'Building a great brand is something you have to be conscious of at all times. You need to constantly challenge everything you're doing to ensure that it's consistent with what it is you want to stand for and be known for, because every activity communicates something about a brand.'

Lessons from product branding

Branding is a bit like creating a theatrical production. Once the stage is set everything contributes to the entire show: the acting, the lighting, the costumes, the programme, the publicity.

Here's a whistle-stop tour of the branding world which will help you understand what's involved when branding yourself, because the principles are the same.

1 A step-by-step process

Going back to that product on the supermarket shelf, branding experts have a specific approach with each product. They:

- declare what it is setting out to achieve (like the Inner Game, its goals define its direction and audience)
- identify what the brand stands for (like the Inner Game, its values are the glue that holds it together)
- declare the brand promise (like being Bloody Good, it shows what it will deliver and how it is distinct).

They then begin expressing it and choose defining words, emotions, colours, images, sounds, objects and behaviour associated with the brand.

Similarly, as individuals, we create our brand using the same process and we express it in our communication, verbal (what we say and do) and non-verbal (our body language, tone of voice, clothes), enabling us to be 'top of mind', the first person people think of.

On a practical level, as consumers, we choose the product because of four things, which map onto the reasons people choose us.

Table 8 ● Choosing the product – and us

Product	Us
Ingredients	Our vision, goals and values: *Inner Game*
Value for money	Our knowledge, experience, skills and competencies and our track record of achievement: *Be Bloody Good*
Packaging	How we look, how we come across, how we communicate: *Turn Up The Volume*
Reputation	Being known and at the forefront of people's minds: *Don't Just Sit There*

2 Sensory branding

According to Martin Lindstrom, the more senses a brand appeals to, the more we remember it.[1] So the experts will build the brand across many senses to make sure they create a strong, positive and loyal bond between it and us. Who can see Andrex toilet paper without feeling warm and fuzzy about that cute puppy? The Coca-Cola brand is so ingrained across sight, emotion, taste and sound (I can hear the sound of 'it's the real thing' as I write) that even if we see just a fragment of a broken bottle, or if the distinctive lettering is used for something else, we can't help but know that it's Coke. That's why we reach unthinkingly for those products on the super-market shelf. Lindstrom believes that the brand building of the future will move from a two-sensory approach (sight and sound) to a multi-sensory approach. Expanding your brand platform to appeal to as many senses as possible makes sense. Think of a coffee shop where you can smell the aroma of the freshly ground coffee; can you walk past without stopping? It's extremely difficult to resist (assuming you like coffee, of course).

The purpose of creating a sensory brand is to add emotional engagement to your brand, creating a strong, positive and loyal bond between you and your audience so that they will turn to you repeatedly and barely notice competitors. By adding more sensory experiences, you get what is known as synergy, or a 2 + 2 = 5 effect. where the whole is greater than the sum of its parts. At Saatchi & Saatchi, the collective noun for this effort is 'sisomo' where you bring together sight, sound and motion.

Sensory branding is mainly built on sight, sound and touch:

- **Sight**, according to Martin Lindstrom, is the most seductive sense of all. It often overrules the other senses and has the power to persuade us against all logic. If you're anything like me, you'll have made many impractical purchases because something looked too good to resist. Sight covers everything from size and shape to clarity and colour.

- **Sound** is connected to our moods and emotions. Filmmakers and brand experts draw on the fact that music can generate feelings and influence our reactions. Imagine the *Jaws* movie without the famous, 'da da' music. Music influences our behaviour, too. When shopping, the slower the music, the more we shop; the faster the pace the less we spend. We spend more time dining when the music is slower. Music is linked to moods and moods are linked to spending.

- **Touch** and feel are words that describe both the physical and the emotional. The feel of fabric or paper and the feelings of comfort or pleasure – we touch and are touched. Companies are catching up with the importance of feelings in a new concept of emotional branding. According to Kevin Roberts, worldwide CEO of Saatchi & Saatchi, and his Lovemarks theory, the best marketing campaigns in the world today are those that make an emotional connection with consumers.[2] 'The role of great marketing is simply this: to inspire loyalty beyond reason,' he argues. 'It's not enough now to be irreplaceable; what you've got to become is irresistible.' A Lovemark brand elicits an emotional response from its customers, as well as providing them with the material benefits they expect. For example, Harley Davidson has little to do with motorbikes and much to do with adventure and freedom. The cheapest Harley is more profitable than the most expensive Suzuki because it is a Lovemark. Roberts argues that consumers are powered by emotion, not by their rational selves. To this end, he added, Saatchi & Saatchi was recently commissioned by Toyota to reposition it from the most respected car brand in the world to the most loved. To illustrate his point, he carried out a survey of American presidents since the war using a quadrant diagram, with love along its x-axis and respect along its y-axis to plot their position.

Who would you guess was the only US president since the war to be high on both love and respect? The answer is Kennedy. Where was Bill Clinton? Bottom-right: low respect, high love, as you would imagine. Arguably George W. Bush would rate low on both.

The 'high respect, low love' zone is where most brands sit. To survive in the future, you need to move to the top-right. In other words, you must become a Lovemark.

Smell and taste are also obviously included in sensory branding too. But as we move on to personal branding, they're harder to include. So beyond the obvious – avoid heavily scented perfumes and aftershaves, and check your personal hygiene – it's best to focus on the others instead.

3 Building brand awareness

Symbols abound in our world and are an important part of building brand recognition. A host of them will come to mind: the HMV dog, the McDonald's golden arches, the Arsenal cannon. As consumers, the objects we choose are also symbols: the Mont Blanc pen, the pink mobile phone, the rubber charity bracelet. On a psychological level we choose things because they symbolise something about us and confirm what's important to us, what kind of home we have, how stylish we are, our health, our economic status and our allegiances. The principle applies in a work context when, for example, we choose good people to work in the team; it also says something about us, perhaps sound judgement, the ability to spot talent, or a commitment to quality.

The aim that branding experts have is to increase the strength of a brand's presence in the consumer's mind,[3] building up through:

- recognition (familiarity)
- recall (being able to bring the brand to mind when prompted)
- 'top of mind' (the first brand recalled)
- dominant (the only brand recalled).

I use these terms as a measure of the effectiveness of a personal brand with the aim of being at least 'top of mind'.

4 Personal brand

People, too, have a uniqueness that can be branded. A personal brand is a promise of performance that creates expectations in its audience. Done well it clearly communicates the values, personality and abilities of the person behind it. It's built on a foundation of confidence, direction and values and is about being comfortable with who you are: there is nothing quite as beautiful as people who are happy to be themselves.

Diana Boulter, of DBA Speakers, has learned to be true to herself. Her brand message sweeps into the room with her – colourful, expressive and passionate with bags of energy. Her work has taught her not to be afraid of people. 'Business people at the top can come across as terrifying to ordinary people not at their level,' she observes. Early on, she taught herself to see people as people and not to be in awe of them. They shop, eat, sleep and make love just like everyone else. They have dreams, concerns and fears just like everyone else. 'I learned that when I am with people I can only be myself: they'll either like me or they won't, but they won't like me more if I pretend to be something I'm not.' She has a healthy respect for them and is genuinely interested in what makes them tick. But equally she has a healthy respect for herself.

So how do we draw on the lessons of product branding when building our own personal brand? First, we need to know what our brand messages are.

How do I stack up?

Take a cashmere-socks moment: it's time to think about yourself as a brand and how you come across to others, so it's a good time to let your thoughts float free. Remember that a cashmere-socks moment is about just going with the flow, day dreaming and listening to the ideas that pop into your mind. Remember, too, that there are no oughts, just what is.

Words and more words

Before we start, remember your favourite object? Get the paper with your list of adjectives. Now put 'I am' in front of each adjective. How close does this come to describing you?

I was speaking once to a group of executive women in London and we had huge fun doing this exercise. One woman in particular stands out in my mind – a colourful, theatrical extrovert. Her object was an enormous dress ring worn on her right hand. What were her words?

I am large
I am showy
I am individual
'That's me down to a tee!' she roared with laughter.

This is a quick and easy way to begin uncovering your brand message.

Now let's add to the three words. For this next exercise, write the first things that pop into your mind, without analysing, defending or filtering.

....

Exercise

Step 1: Make a list

Taking no more than two minutes for each category, list as many words as you can think of that:

1   **You** would use to describe you.
2   Your **boss** would use to describe you.
3   Your **peers** would use to describe you.
4   Your **team members** would use to describe you.
5   Your **clients** would use to describe you.
6   Your **friends** would use to describe you.
7   Your **family** would use to describe you.
8   A **brand expert** would use to describe you.

You can add or ignore categories to tailor this list to the 'touch points' (people on the receiving end) of your brand.

Step 2: Review your list

Look at your words and tidy the list up a bit.

1   Do any words say the same thing? For example, you may have words like warm, friendly and open that could be summarised in one word.

2   Do any themes appear?

If you've listed words such as honest, integrity and fair, they are all examples of values. If you've listed words such as strategic, organised, analytical, practical and good at selling, they are all examples of strengths. If you've listed words such as exciting, motivating, reassuring and supportive, they are all examples of emotions you inspire.

Step 3: Reflect on the messages that emerge from your list

● Are there clashes between your words and the words others use about you? Do you think you're clear, but others perceive you as verbose?

● Are there differences between the words that different groups of people use? Do your colleagues perceive you as fun but your boss describes you as shy?

● What is causing the differences?

A rule of thumb here is that perception is reality: whether it's true or not, the way others perceive you is what counts. We tend to judge ourselves by our intentions; I may intend to be warm and friendly but if my team perceive me as haughty and aloof, then that's what I am for them.

Step 4: Can you add more words to your list?

Before reviewing how you express and communicate your brand, use these last questions to see whether there are words you have not yet chosen and that should be added:

● What are the brands associated with me? Why? What are the words they bring to mind?

● Which admired person (or character) is like me? Why?

● What is my marketplace? What do I know about it and where do I interact with it (what are the touch points: face to face;

presentations; e-mail; voicemail; conference calls; strategy papers)?

- What's the recall factor? What do people recall about me?
- How does my brand make others feel?
- What are the strengths and values that distinguish me?
- What makes me useful to others?
- How do I compare with others? How am I better than others?

Step 5: Finalise your list

Distil all the words into a summary list of the words that best describe you.

If we were doing this for Lisa Fabian Lustigman, the family lawyer from Withers, the brand words that scream out are: forthright; firm; direct; New Yorker; stylish and classy; confident and authoritative; warm and witty. Her brand touches people in meetings, in the office, in e-mails, in court, in letters, in legal documents, on the phone, at networking events and conferences.

Considering your list of words that describe the 'what' and 'where' of your brand, the next step is to reflect on how you express and package your brand in a way that is authentic and natural for you. Look at your summary list as you begin to populate Table 9. The categories in the quadrants are suggestions only, to prompt your thinking. So, don those cashmere socks and begin reflecting.

The descriptors of Adam Oliver of BT's brand include quirky, engaging, sincere, inclusive, generous in praise, passionate, witty, and self-deprecating:

> My brand is more about what others perceive, not what I do; it's important for me to manage that perception. Quirkiness makes your brand memorable, and here's one of my favourite quirky ways. My mum makes superbly wonderful chocolate cakes and flapjacks which are

Table 9 ● Sight, touch/feel, sound, symbols

Sight

Visual elements of your brand include:

Your clothes – classic or dramatic?

Your colours – bright or muted?

Your size – statuesque or dainty?

Your shape – lean or portly?

Your hairstyle – shaven or cascading?

Your handwriting – spider scrawl or artistic?

Your presentations – words or pictures?

Your body language- open or skulking?

Your logo – abstract or literal?

What else?

Sound

Auditory elements of your brand include:

The sound of your voice – mellifluous or high pitched?

Intonation – flat or undulating?

The words you use – colourful or measured?

Your accent – *Corrie* or pukka?

Your expressions – colloquial or formal?

Your ring tone – 'Crazy Frog' or 'Greensleeves'?

What else?

Touch/feel

Include both touch and feelings:

Your handshake – knuckle-breaker or limp?

Your pace – hare or tortoise?

Your textures – cashmere or woven?

Your writing paper – heavy or smooth?

The emotions you generate - Excitement or fun?

Warmth or inspiration?

Energy or calm?

Symbols

The symbols we choose symbolise something about us:

Your perfume – are you classy Chanel or fresh Jo Malone?

Your watch – are you youthful Swatch or James Bond Omega?

Your glasses – are you funky Versace or practical Boots own?

Your pens – are you substantial Mont Blanc or colourful biro?

Your jewellery/cufflinks – are you establishment Asprey's or up to the minute Primark?

Your car – are you in-front Toyota or funky Beetle?

Your drink – are you a sociable Guinness or sparkling Bolly?

The list goes on – your holiday, your restaurant, your sport, your home.

Some people cultivate their own distinctive features: ties, hats, earrings, etc.

What else?

What else?

> shared around BT. In return, my senior manager's wife
> also bakes me pumpkin bread and this became a talking
> point: how come you get pumpkin bread from the boss's
> wife?

Adam's mother's baking is now well known and a frequent topic of conversation.

Now that you have the descriptors of your brand, the next step is to decide how best to communicate it.

What do I do?

Think about Brighton rock for a moment. At some time we've probably all bought some of the sugary pink candy sticks sold in seaside towns everywhere. The centre of the stick is white and has a message written in a contrasting colour, something humorous, perhaps 'kiss me quick' or 'I love mum', or the name of the resort, perhaps Brighton. The point is, wherever you break that stick of rock, you see the same message at its core. Brands need to learn the Brighton rock lesson as consistency forms a large part in building brand loyalty; to be believable, the message must be congruent everywhere, aligned with each touch point. Your brand must be the yardstick against which all your communication, behaviours and actions are measured. It cannot be a simple collection of words and phrases: it must be visible, tangible and all-embracing. Thinking about company branding, a van with a logo cutting us up on the road, a grumpy receptionist reluctant to help or a grubby display shelf all make an incongruent impression in the consumer's mind.

So what does incongruent look like for us? It's the technical director, an off-the-planet creative genius, and a true visionary, who sends long, technical e-mails to busy people who are not terribly interested. Instead of seeing genius, people experience his brand as irritating and out of touch. It's the strategist with a razor-sharp brain and a rare talent for analysis who works in mess and chaos, her desk barely visible under the piles of papers waiting to be filed. Instead of seeing clarity, people experience her brand as muddled and confused. Mess or crabby e-mails are not wrong in themselves and may be part of a brand, too. They only become a problem when they get in the way and distract people from what you want them to think about you. Simply being aware of what you're doing and how you come across is the best possible start for any change you want to make.

Your brand is deeper than its packaging. Cast your mind back to the Inner Game and Be Bloody Good, and remember that the stuffed mushrooms, frog goals and signature strengths all make up the passion of the brand. Notice how Adam Oliver's brand exudes passion, which is followed through in his actions.

....

The man who attracts nice people

Adam Oliver of BT is so passionate about his work and the potential it has to improve lives that he frequently gets emotional and wells up when he talks about what he does. 'If you can change things for one person, you can change it for thousands.' Here's just one example: a random meeting with Mesar, a blind man who said that he couldn't pick up text messages because he couldn't see them, inspired Adam to get his researchers on the case, to work creatively to come up with a solution. That's how BT's message to landline was born.

Adam is also passionate about developing people, evidenced in his active mentoring of BT apprentices. He believes in nurturing the next generation of talent and loves being able to influence young people's lives. His involvement with the apprentices came about when by chance he met an apprentice and, as is his wont, got involved and organised BT Research Labs visits for him and his friends. From that small beginning Adam got hooked and went on to create a formal programme for mentoring apprentices.

Adam seeks out talent among the apprentice group and mentors between 12 and 20 of them. Hence Ben Taylor, Adam Brown and Harry Jones, his 'Three Musketeers', were with him when we met. He encourages them to speak out, involving and praising them constantly. So what do his mentees say about him? 'It's a bit of a shock to the system when a senior manager includes us, and doesn't treat us as the bottom of the pile. Adam is approachable and welcoming, informal and non-hierarchical, and he opens doors for us.' In a potentially hierarchical jungle this is highly unusual. Adam brings them into meetings and exposes them to different parts of the business. For example, he included two of them in a directors' meeting and invited them to participate. Their input brought the meeting alive and added a valuable perspective; so much so that having new people present at these meetings has now become the norm for this group. This gives the apprentices confidence to remove barriers for themselves. It is things like this that enhance Adam's reputation, too.

Adam is not hugely driven to climb the corporate ladder and move up the hierarchy. Instead he prefers to co-ordinate activities across teams with an open reach to people to get a result. Knowing himself, and knowing what he's passionate about, he knows exactly what to opt into and what to opt out of.

Values are also deeply ingrained in a personal brand and tell us what the person stands for. In the case of Dyfrig James of Lafarge, safety is the Brighton rock message that runs through his core. Notice particularly how his actions and behaviour are all consistent with his values and how he 'walks the talk'.

The Welshman who wears red socks

Dyfrig James has a personal brand that is characterised by his large personality, self-deprecating humour and bright red socks; you are captivated immediately. I first met him on a videoconference, and even though the image was blurred, his brand managed to defy technological limits, to jump out from the screen and make an impression. When you look deeper into his brand, you'll see that a passion for safety is at its core. This stems right back to his early days as managing director of Lafarge's Aggregates and Concrete business. Weeks after he took over in 2003, Dyfrig was informed of a fatality in one of their quarries. One of the most experienced quarrymen, a loyal employee with over 40 years of service, had died in a rock-face collapse in one of the quarries. Dyfrig immediately went down to the quarry to talk to his co-workers. Hugging grown men in tears through shock and grief, he realised that something drastic would have to be done. Visiting the family in mourning, he knew with a deep certainty that safety had to be his number one priority from then on: he didn't want to be responsible for more deaths.

So his trademark 'Visible, Felt, Leadership' was born; a brand of leadership that walks the talk, that lives and breathes safety every single moment of every single day. He took his message all round the company, communicating to everyone that safety was a number one priority, that the goal was zero incidents and that he would be taking a hard line with anyone breaking the rules. No one believed him. But only two years later, the safety record was the best the company had ever achieved, and now people believe him. When the first target was achieved, Dyfrig gave everyone a day off to celebrate. He constantly recognises achievements and progress made, usually with a safety-related gift. On one occasion, he gave an MP3 player as a reward; on it was his safety message. A few days later he was touched to receive a letter from the son of the recipient, who'd heard the message and wanted to thank Dyfrig for keeping his dad safe.

When asked specifically about what he does to convey his brand message, the safety part comes easily. But what about the red socks? Well, red is dynamic, and the colour of his homeland – and he's proud of his Welsh heritage; they're bright and cheerful; they're different and they stand out. The words fit Dyfrig perfectly.

In my experience, people are magnetically drawn to the opportunity of understanding and expressing their brand. It seems to whet the appetites of Tarzans and Janes across the board. It's essentially a simple process. Once we understand the essence of our brand, we can set about intentionally communicating it verbally (what we say, do and deliver) and non-verbally (our body language, tone of voice, clothes), getting to be 'top of mind'.

Before we start, have you come across these percentages before: 7%, 38% and 55%? Surprisingly, according to Professor Albert Mehrabian, only 7% of communication is made up of language and the words used, and 38% is made up of the sound of our voice, the pace, the intonation and the tone. This leaves 55%, which means that by far the biggest and most influential is our non-verbal communication.[4] For effective and meaningful communication, these three parts of the message need to support each other in meaning – they have to be congruent. In case of any incongruency, the receiver of the message might be irritated by two messages coming from two different channels, giving cues in two different directions. The 55% covers sight and body language; smell; symbols; actions and behaviour. Arguably one of the world's most successful personal brands was Princess Diana. Her iconic image as the people's princess – with descriptors like informal, accessible, fashionable, glamorous, maternal, caring, sexy, coy, unhappy, emotional – was based almost entirely on the 55%, non-verbal communication; we only rarely heard her speak.

This section shows you how to express your Brighton rock message by fine-tuning the communication of your brand in terms of your language, voice and non-verbal cues.

What do I do?

1 Communicating the brand through language

Words are powerful tools and choosing the right ones is a skill that everyone can develop. The art lies in knowing which

Table 10 ● Linguistic devices

Old	New
Hedge your bets with words like 'maybe', 'perhaps', 'I have a problem with this report'	I disagree with this report
Use disclaimers like 'I may be wrong but'	This is my opinion
Use tag questions which appear at the end of the sentence: 'I think this is the best way to do this, don't you?'	I think this is the best way to do this
Couch statements as questions: 'Could we go for the second option?'	I endorse the second option
Use self-deprecation: 'I'm probably not the best person to answer that'	From my experience, I recommend that

words to choose and which to avoid. When we discuss this at seminars, the general consensus is that there are no absolute rules, only guidelines, and the driving concern should always be to build rapport and to be natural. The last thing people want to be is overly contrived with their language. We also agree that awareness and listening to role models speak, followed by preparation, are the best ways to build new language habits, to become fluent and articulate. With being natural firmly in mind, here are a few tips about language.

Linguistic devices

Checking back to Jane's favoured linguistic devices from He, she, me, we for a moment, we saw that in Tarzan's world they contribute to an impression that Jane is indecisive. Table 10 lists a few alternative suggestions to adapt to your own personal style.

Jane's style is generally very effective in influencing and engaging others, so only adapt where it is affecting your impact negatively.

Fresh language

Like everything else, use of language should be context and personality driven. As an example, the ubiquitous word 'awesome' works fine in the United States but doesn't go down quite so well in the European corporate jungle, and certainly doesn't sit well with a traditional British style.

Using strong fresh language increases the impact of your brand. Tables 11 and 12 give suggestions for increasing your word power.

Table 11 ● Increase your word power

Old	New
Good	Great, outstanding, (awesome)
Relevant	Pivotal, germane
Big	Massive, powerful, significant
Completed	Fulfilled, delivered, realised
New	Leading edge, fresh, innovative

Adapted from Mary Spillane, *Branding Yourself*, Pan Books, 2000

It's best to avoid corporate speak. Modern business speak should be clear, not convoluted. Taking the long way round to explain something or speaking in jargon will impress few. The most influential speakers are clear and economic with words.

Engaging language

Adam Oliver, of BT, engages people by telling stories: about his chocolate cakes and pumpkin bread; about a blind man who couldn't read text messages. Stories and metaphors, similes and parables make us listen and get us to remember the message long after. They are useful devices that allow us to step aside from the main message, helping us to understand

Table 12 ● Words to avoid/preferred words

Words to avoid	Preferred words
Why is a loaded word; it sounds aggressive and almost assumes the worst. 'Why did you decide that?' A question that starts with the word why invites justification rather than information.	Use 'how', 'what', 'when', 'where' or 'who' instead to gain useful information For instance, 'what were the deciding factors?'
Should is another loaded word. It invariably has judgement or blame attached to it. When you tell someone that they should do something, you introduce a parent–child transaction that invites compliance or rebellion rather than engagement.	Use words that open up possibilities and involve others. 'What do you think?' 'Could we do this?' 'My suggestion is this.' Jane language can be useful, don't you think?
But (and *however*) make all the words that precede them worthless. 'Well done, that was really good, but you need to include more detail' negates all the praise that comes before.	Substitute 'but' with 'and' to provide constructive feedback: 'Well done, that was really good, and more detail will make it even more effective in future.'
Try is about effort not accomplishment so to try is ultimately to fail. 'I tried' is almost always an excuse and is 'poor me' language. When we say that we will try, what we really mean is that we are not committed to the result.	'I will do this by next Wednesday.' 'I am not prepared to commit to this deadline because my current project must take priority. What I can do is to get it to you by next month.'
'*Don't* think of a pink elephant.' You have to think of the pink elephant in order not to think about it. Don't forget Don't be afraid Don't worry about finding this difficult	Use positive statements rather than negative instructions. Remember Be confident; you'll enjoy this You'll find this easy and straightforward

by expressing the message in different way. 'Being a CEO is a bit like conducting an orchestra; you pull everyone together to produce a beautiful symphony.' The business world is drenched in metaphor: cash flow; liquid assets; floating a company; going out and grabbing the market; defeating the opposition; wooing the customer.

Here are some suggestions for adding colour:

- Listen to people speak and take note of the way they use language. Compare the language of someone impressive and someone who generally fails to impress. What do you notice?

- Find a good role model and listen to a speech repeatedly until you absorb the language patterns, like learning a song.

- Build a repertoire of stories and use them in your conversations.

- Use a trademark word or phrase to be memorable, such as Sharon Osborne's 'fabulous' or Sherlock Holmes's 'elementary'.

- Prepare in advance and ask yourself – what do I want to say? What is this like? What else explains it? Is it clear and fresh?

Influential language

We've seen that people have favourite ways of processing information by seeing, hearing, feeling or analysing. There are more ways that we use to process information. Understanding and using them will add a dash of sophistication to your influencing skills.

- **Big chunk, small chunk.** Some people want the big picture, while others want detail. You lose your audience when you fail to recognise which system you're talking to. I was once working with a highly technical product manager for CISCO, helping him prepare a presentation for a group of senior leaders. He showed me his 78 PowerPoint slides filled with hundreds of words, explaining his project in the tiniest detail. He would have been dead in seconds. Adam Oliver advises: simplify your message; use a few pictures or graphs and talk to these. You can always have the detail prepared and be able to answer questions for those who want it. However, if you're attending a conference full of technical experts, they are likely to want the substance and detailed methodology of your ideas so make sure you don't fob them off with too little information; they will perceive your big picture presentation as superficial.

- **Necessity, possibility.** Some people process ideas according to what's possible, while others are interested in what needs to be done. Are you working to express yourself or because you need to pay the mortgage? Or both? To the possibility person, you talk about opportunities, what's out there, what can be created, blue-sky thinking. To the necessity person, you talk about how your ideas meet the need to meet deadlines, to pay creditors, to bring in new revenue, to deliver the pipeline of new products.

- **Same, different.** Some people like things to stay the same, while others rush towards change, embracing it with open arms. I have a friend who moves house every couple of years and in between moves, she arranges and rearranges furniture almost daily. You need to check carefully before you sit down, as the chair is rarely where you thought it would be. Leaders who introduce change initiative on top of change initiative on top of change initiative can leave people confused and weary. At work, change oriented people will change companies often, or at least roles within the same company; you'll retain people when you recognise this. In pitching ideas to a 'same' person, you'd suggest that your solution is 'pretty much the same as you're doing now, with just a couple of enhancements', or 'this won't be new to you; you're already using some of the principles'. By contrast, a 'different' person will want to hear that 'this is a fresh new approach; a radical departure from what we've already done'.

- **Towards, away from.** What is motivating your next move? Are you moving towards a new job or away from what you dislike in the old one? People are motivated towards something they want or away from something they want to avoid. We may be motivated towards wealth or away from poverty, towards success or away from failure. In pitching an idea, you'd talk about the benefits of taking on your idea and how you'll protect the business from risks. 'This new system will offer us speedier customer delivery times and will improve our service.' Or: 'This new system will prevent us losing our customers to the competition because of our poor service levels.'

You may be wondering, 'What if I don't know people's preferred ways to process information?' It's a good question. You may well be talking to people you've never met before or, indeed, to a group of people who have different preferences. Tuning into their language and how they express themselves gradually is the only way to do it. Otherwise, you'll need to include different styles when speaking. It's perfectly accept-able to say, 'I'll give an overview first and then I'll give the details for those who prefer more information', or, 'enough of the details for now, let's take the helicopter view'.

- **You and I.** The most compelling speakers use the words 'you' and 'we' more than the word 'I'. Changing the focus of speech from self to others is more influential. 'What do you think', rather than 'let me tell you what I think'.

Written language

I love George Orwell's questions; they've become my golden rules for written language. 'A scrupulous writer, in every sentence that he writes, will ask himself at least four questions: What am I trying to say? What words will express it? What image or idiom will make it clearer? Is this image fresh enough to have an effect?'

All the principles about influencing through language apply here too; and here are more useful hints and tips:

- Provide a clear structure – purpose, what's the outcome; focus, what are the issues to address; summary, what are the key points and what are the next steps.
- Start with the big picture and then go into detail.
- Avoid long sentences.
- Remember the importance of good grammar and punctuation; it still counts.

2 *Communicating the brand through sound*

One of my favourite TV presenters is Fiona Bruce, a BBC newsreader. I can listen to her for hours without needing to hear a word she says, mesmerised by the timbre of her voice, its pitch and intonation, the pace and timing of her delivery. Listening to her, it's easy to remember that 38% of our brand is communicated through its sound. There was a major problem for some stars of the silent screen: their looks were at odds with the sounds of their voices as they made the transition to talking movies. In the classic movie *Singing in the Rain*, Lina Lamont had to be dubbed by Kathy Seldon, someone who could sing and talk beautifully. Of course, Lina ultimately got what she deserved; her false pretences were exposed and

Kathy got her recognition. I'm sure that none of us are quite as dire as the ill-fated Ms Lamont, but there are still ways to improve the sound of our brand.

The first thing you need to do is to listen to yourself. Record something you've recently spoken about at work. Play the tape back. How do you sound? What impact do you have? What kind of person do you sound like? What values do you think people pick up when they hear you? How energising is your message? Ask your mentor, coach, or respected colleague to give you additional feedback.

Here's a second exercise: record two more messages. First, talk about something you passionately believe in, something you know a lot about. How do you express yourself? Second, talk about something that bores you, or something you are unsure about. How do you express yourself? What's the difference?

You can now model your own excellence, building on the qualities of your first recording. By using this style more and more, those qualities become habit. Speak 'as if' you are always you at your most passionate and certain.

A couple of years ago I coached a highly successful and competent senior bank executive in Singapore. He wanted to increase his influencing skills, realising that although he was passionate and knowledgeable, his message was couched in a rather monotonous voice, with little variation in pace, tone or pitch; so rather than engaging people, they found it hard to listen to him. We found two simple ways to improve his delivery. Just by smiling more, he lifted the sound of his voice, lightened his message and drew people in. If you're trying this out, don't overdo it – you risk being like the dour Malvolio in *Twelfth Night* who tried out unnatural and exaggerated smiling, thinking this was the secret of winning his mistress's heart.

The second thing the bank executive did was to identify a role model; in his case it was the CEO. The task was to select

Table 13 ● Improve your sound

What	How
To add energy	Vary the pace; add depth and volume.
To add expression	Move facial muscles; smile; vary the intonation.
To sound more positive	Add volume and depth; use pauses; emphasise words and phrases. Watch how much you use padding words, such as like, um, you know. Use emotion.
To sound more articulate	Prepare and be clear; avoid jargon; improve your vocabulary; look up new words as you read; resist the urge to think out loud.

a speech he'd made and listen to it repeatedly, until he could hear the patterns and cadences in his head. Consciously at first, then unconsciously, he began to match the sound, letting it influence his own sound patterns. He still sounded like himself; there was simply more movement and colour to his voice.

There are places to go to for help in improving your sound. Many, including politicians, use voice coaches to add impact. Margaret Thatcher's voice deepened over time, gaining an authority that served her well. Acting classes are a great place to improve not only voice, but also movement and improvisation; there you will be taught about breathing and projection which will add depth and volume to your voice.

Table 13 provides a few general hints and tips.

Some final points to be aware of:

● Raising our voice at the end of a sentence is usually perceived as a question (typical of Janes). Keeping our voice level is usually perceived as a statement. Dropping our voice down at the end of a sentence is usually perceived as an order.

● In a telephone conversation, matching the other person's voice will help build rapport. A few years ago, I overheard a woman in my team on the telephone to one of her clients. I noticed that she was practically whispering down the phone. After her conversation, I went over to her and asked, 'Elaine, why did you speak so quietly? It's not like you.' She told me, 'The client speaks so quietly that he doesn't hear me if I speak loudly.' Incidentally, she was the most successful sales person.

● Different accents needn't be a problem: just make sure you are clear, check for understanding and keep your mouth clear so people can also lip read.

3 Communicating the brand through non-verbal cues

Body language, behaviour, clothes: these make up the final and most influential part, the 55%, of the brand.

Body language

A few years ago, I went for some leadership coaching with my sales director. Our coach believed in tough empathy and didn't hold back when giving us feedback. To demonstrate a point, at one stage he mirrored the body language I was using, quite unconsciously, at meetings. I watched in horror as he put his elbows on the table, rested his head in his hands, gave a little smile and tilted his head submissively to the right. Although Janes have a tendency to use softer body language, what I saw mirrored was the body language of a Jane at her least powerful. I was mortified. What I was feeling inside was strong, focused, ambitious and energised. That's incongruence for you. It was one of the best pieces of feedback I've ever had. I now make a conscious effort to use squarer body language in business meetings. Princess Diana used the coy look, tilting her head to one side, but in her case it was a way to build rapport and to be liked and was not incongruent. Awareness of your body language is essential in ensuring your brand messages are congruent. The best way to learn how you come across is to watch yourself on camera. I must admit I find this a pretty horrific experience, but once you get over the shock, it's a great way to see what you're really doing rather than what you think you're doing. It's also good to be courageous and seek feedback from someone willing to tell you what you need to know rather than what you want to hear.

The suggestions I'm touching on here to improve your body language are remarkably simple, and the proverbial grandmothers and eggs may come to mind, but experience tells me that what is common sense is rarely common practice.

- **Use grounded physiology.** We have seen that adopting grounded physiology can help build confidence. It is also a way of conveying a confident, natural and aligned brand without saying a word. This is what I mean by grounded physiology: stand squarely with upright posture; relax your shoulders and pull them back; breathe deeply from your diaphragm. Relax your facial muscles, look around calmly, and stand firmly on your legs.

- **Smile.** Contrary to W.C. Fields's observation, 'start off every day with a smile and get it over with', real smiling is another way to change your state instantly, change the response you get. And it can be a positive way of building the right kind of rapport with people.

- **Use good posture.** Though I hope you're not thinking 'she sounds like my mother', good posture makes a huge difference to how you come across. Visiting my father-in-law in his retirement home, I loved to look around at the other residents and couldn't help but notice what a huge impact good posture had on how old people looked. My favourite posture-improvers are:

- Alexander technique, which lets the body re-learn its natural stance
- Pilates, which helps build a strong set of core muscles to support the back
- Dance, so much more fun than keep-fit classes and just look at the posture of dancers
- Martial arts, which I'm told is amazing. Just watch Bruce Lee in action – no round shoulders there.

One guru[5] suggests that you imagine you're a cat and that will transform your posture; I tried it out and got one or two strange looks as I slunk about, but it worked.

My overriding advice is to be aware, to be in rapport with the person or people you are with and to be natural, and your body language won't be far wrong.

Behaviour

What people do and how they behave counts for more than what they say, no matter how passionate and articulate the message. The worst leader I've come across was outstanding at rhetoric, with presentation skills to die for. He would give rousing talks about the importance of people to the success of the business, and about his role in providing the support and encouragement people would need to succeed. How he inspired! But when it came down to it, he would cancel meetings, give people the silent treatment, avoid dealing with difficult situations and subject people to outbursts of his volatile temper. Trust was broken, his words seen to be empty were no longer believed; this was an incongruent brand in action.

To avoid the empty rhetoric syndrome, always mean what you say and follow through.

Behaviour can be a distinguishing feature of your brand and can add to your reputation. I discovered this when I was assessing business development consultants for a client with a view to providing meaningful and personalised development plans for each. I came across Natalie O'Neill, who consistently wowed clients by going way over and above any levels of service they had ever experienced. You could describe her Bloody Good brand of client focus as over-delivery, speedy response times, rigorous follow-up, meticulous delivery, adding value – all captured by the Japanese term *miryokuteki hinshitsu*, which means above and beyond the expected quality. But even this wouldn't quite capture it. Natalie described a time when she happened to be in the major retail store of one of her clients in her spare time. She took note of her shopping experiences, watched how things were done and saw where opportunities were being missed. The next day, she contacted the managing director and gave him a creative and hugely constructive report that would add significantly to his revenue. He was well and truly wowed. In just this way, a Bloody Good strength, followed through with congruent behaviour, becomes part of a Brighton rock brand.

Clothes

The story goes that someone once approached a well-known chairman and CEO of a major corporation, admiring how she looked. 'How do you do it?' she was asked. 'You always look amazing, so on the money. What's your secret?' The CEO reflected for a moment and gave her answer: 'Just two words,' she said; 'Giorgio. Armani.'

Clothes (not only Armani), cosmetics and accessories are the packaging of the brand and play a massive part in creating the four-second message that tells others about us. How we look is a subject close to the hearts of many and has spawned a huge industry abounding with retailers jostling to entice us, makeover programmes, books and magazines, consultants and A-list style gurus. The luxury goods market in the United States alone generates revenues in excess of $12 billion.[6] Designer accoutrements can certainly add cachet, but they don't guarantee style and are not always the answer. The secret is to know yourself, and make sure that you wear the clothes rather than let the clothes wear you. We've got it just about right when people notice us before the clothes. 'You look great' rather than 'what designer is your watch or suit or bag or tie?'.

It's important to strike the right balance between taking advice and being yourself. Breaking new ground as one of the first female directors in the telecoms industry, Deb Covey of BT was not given any guidance about appropriate business attire. She was 29 when she was first promoted to director, the only female on the team. A young and energetic Jane, she eagerly prepared for her first off-site management meeting. She agonised over what to wear, finally settling on a beautiful red suit. As she entered the meeting room, a sea of navy and grey-suited men confronted her. She stood out like a sore thumb in her red: some loved it, some looked askance, and there were some 'tsk tsks' over her poor judgement. She was initially uncomfortable and self-conscious, but then thought, 'You know what? I am different and putting on a black suit won't hide that; it is what it is.' She believes that people entering the corporate jungle should be given some basic advice. After that it's important to be you, forget about clothes and get on with the task at hand.

The aim is to express your brand and be comfortable with your image. Strict rules and cloning are to be avoided, but at the same time getting your look sorted out and looking the part will make sure that you're credible and current.

After a speaking engagement at CISCO, an attractive man wearing a funky ponytail and earrings approached me to talk about his image. He was quite comfortable and happy with himself, yet he realised that how he looked would create barriers for him in his new client-facing role. We worked out that his ponytail and earrings were his way of reflecting his brand of being different, original and creative. So what he did was to find other, more subtle ways of expressing this, for example with funky cuff links and watch, which would allow him to enter his clients' world and build credibility and rapport while still reflecting his brand.

Most of us are not so good at knowing what suits us best, and if you're anything like me you'll need a little help through the maze. What's my best style: glamorous or natural; chic or trendy; dramatic or elegant? What colours and lines are best for me? What scale and proportion suit my frame? What brands will reflect my personality?

Where is the advice to be found?

- Read magazines for plenty of inexpensive advice.
- Look in shops and try things on with a critical eye. If you shop well with someone else, ask for feedback. By the way, this never works for me.
- Look at people with similar body shape and see what they're wearing.
- Consult a great image coach. Apart from the tough empathy, it is great fun and very self-affirming. The way to justify the cost is to think about how much you'll save by not making those expensive mistakes still hanging untouched in the wardrobe.

Surely this only applies to Janes? Not at all – you'd be surprised how many Tarzans have image coaches. I recently worked with a group of medal-winning male athletes who were in transition to a new role, away from the Olympic limelight towards becoming leaders and spokesmen for their sport. As part of their transition, they needed to get out of their tracksuits and don a more urbane and authoritative look, so I introduced a wonderful image coach to them. The sparks flew as all came up for scrutiny and tough empathy. Collars, cuffs, jackets, shoes, hair and glasses were ruthlessly examined; nothing escaped her sharp but sympathetic eye. They had huge fun and dramatically depleted Austin Reed's stock. Lessons were learned and the 'before and after' pictures were dramatic: they looked and felt absolutely fabulous in their new gear.

As well as projecting an image, clothes can definitely affect how you feel: remember how Mo Mowlam put on her best suit to act 'as if' confident for the bankers? Many of us have favourite suits, lucky dresses, winning ties. A client recently told me that she always gets a result when she wears green. So clothes are a great way to anchor a good feeling and help set the scene for success.

A final word about cost. There are so many wonderful clothes available from all sources. Here are three thoughts:

- High street fashion offers stylish, affordable clothes and you don't have to be dripping in designer to look good.
- Classic designer clothes are generally of a superb quality and last for ages. Buy them in sales or in second-hand stores where you can get hardly worn couture for low prices.
- My favourite justification for designer purchases is to divide the cost by the number of times I will wear them over the coming years and I end up with a no-brainer, a 'must have', 'can't miss' opportunity.

Turn Up The Volume: conclusion

Product branding teaches us about identifying and fine-tuning our core messages: what we stand for, what we deliver and what we communicate verbally and non-verbally. You've explored creative ways of communicating your brand across differ-ent senses and across different touch points so that you are always congruent in everything you do and so that you build a message that gets remembered: in other words, a Brighton rock message, which is woven into language, sound and non-verbal communication. This helps us to influence the perceptions people have of us, and gets us to be 'top of mind' when choices are made. The lessons are there for Tarzans and Janes alike for defining individuality and broadcasting who you are; both need to make an impact. By now, you've looked inside and built clarity, direction and confidence; you've clarified your distinguishing strengths; and you've worked out how to package it all to manage perceptions of you. Now all that remains is to get into the limelight and move centre-stage.

What do I do now?

Here's a quick reminder of what you did before. As you went through the exercises and read about the role models, as you took cashmere-socks moments of reflective thinking, you will have absorbed and integrated some of your insights already so you need take no further conscious action.

- Reread the Making it stick section at the beginning of the book (page xxii); the suggestions apply equally to all the themes and will show you what to do step-by-step.

- If you are curious to learn more, take a look at the What if I want to do more? section at the back (page 188) for resources to help you on your way.

- Get started!

Don't Just Sit There

Overview

The only thing to do with good advice is to pass it on. It's never any use to oneself.

Oscar Wilde

Many people, often Janes, take a passive approach to being discovered and recognised; they sit and wait for a fairy god-mother to send them to the ball. This just won't cut it in the corporate jungle; it doesn't happen like that. 'Don't Just Sit There' is about putting your head above the parapet and being visible, about positive and enjoyable networking. It takes all that you've distilled from the Inner Game and being Bloody Good and is the last part of the branding process begun in Turn Up The Volume. To return to the product metaphor, it's to get the product known and out there with a great reputa-tion, and it's the last of the four themes that make up the blueprint for success.

Strategic networking has been identified as one of the key ingredients for success in the 21st century; deals are made, business is done and jobs are found through contacts. And yet too many of us are woefully negligent when it comes to building our networks. Research tells us that Janes do not use networking as effectively as men and forge fewer important connections. My experience tells me that Tarzans also woefully neglect it.

This section sets the record straight about what networking is not and moves towards an appealing and realistic definition of what it really is. Strategic networking, both inside and outside the organisation, is much more in line with the Jane style of building relationships. It's about information exchange and collaboration, about support and contact, about listening and engaging.

Drawing extensively on lessons learned from successful networkers, this section is relevant whether you're a sophisticated networker, a reluctant networker, or don't know where to begin. It invites you to create your own brand of connecting with others, and what's up for grabs is a live community of enthusiastic people who will help you on your way as you help them on theirs.

The art of strategic networking

What's in it for me?

Having a thriving community of people that you reach out to and who reach out to you will reap rewards in terms of advancing careers, getting new clients, learning new things and getting jobs. This is what Sarah Deaves, CEO of Coutts, has done:

> I built a strong network right from the beginning. I made sure I built my reputation and had the right amount of what I call 'air cover', so that people know me and know what I can do. I also make sure my team get noticed for the contribution they make. That way, I've always been sought out for new opportunities.

Having an approach that you're comfortable with will help you succeed by your own definition on your own terms. No tricks, no gimmicks, no manipulation – this approach invites you to simply be yourself connecting with people in an authentic way.

The good news

The newly defined, demystified way of looking at networking as connecting will get you feeling much more relaxed and natural about the whole thing. As you get out there, you might actually have fun and find that it's much easier than you first thought. Your approach can be entirely tailored around your own personality and brand; the hints and tips are fluid, flexible and mouldable to suit you.

What's it all about?

Before we begin, I have a confession to make: I am a reluctant networker. Given the choice of a night out at a networking conference or an evening in with *Desperate Housewives*, Wisteria Lane will win every time. Given the choice of a good novel or a book about improving my networking, the good novel will win every time. Given the chance to scintillate at a party or a quiet dinner and good conversation with one or two people, the quiet dinner will win every time. I know I'm not alone in being a reluctant networker.

On the one hand, networking is considered to be a crucial ingredient for success. On the other hand, many people neglect it and it remains a seriously underutilised and misunderstood skill, with too many myths in the way. Many people dislike networking because they see it as a rather devious, almost manipulative art of using people and dropping them when they no longer have anything to offer. Who wants to be good at that? That's the first myth. Those who use other people are not the most effective. Successful networking is almost the opposite: it's about naturally connecting to people, building relationships and helping others without necessarily seeking a direct return. Janes are typically good at this. People then want to work with you because they know and trust you.

People typically use these reasons for avoiding networking:

- I have no time to get to things.
- I'm not an extrovert.
- I don't like false conversations with people.
- I don't like 'working a room'.

These seem to presuppose that networking is about attending large gatherings and 'working a room' full of strangers. That's the second myth. Networking is more to do with connecting; it's a particular mindset and ongoing behaviour rather than a specific event. Networking happens anywhere and everywhere, inside and outside the organisation. It might be over an espresso in your company coffee shop, at Weight Watchers, at your wine-tasting class or at a school governors meeting.

Lastly, there's a belief that you need to be an extrovert to be a successful networker. That's the third myth. The truth is that it's much more about being yourself and finding your own style, whether you're an extrovert, an introvert or somewhere in between. I like the terms 'woo' and 'relator' in this context.[1] You may have strong woo characteristics, enjoying the challenge of meeting new people and getting them to like you; you may enjoy initiating conversations with strangers and find strangers energising. Or you may have relator strengths, being pulled towards people you know, deliberately encouraging a deepening of the relationship, wanting to understand their feelings, their goals, their fears, their dreams. You may even be what Malcolm Gladwell calls a connector,[2] one of those few people who seem to know a huge number of other people; someone who acts as a hub for connecting people together.

These different definitions highlight the fact that there isn't one way and it doesn't much matter which category you fit into. They also emphasise that you don't need to copy someone else's way; rather you should focus on developing your own signature style and figuring out what suits you best, because everyone is unique.

Once I realised what the myths surrounding networking were and saw a new definition, I realised that I was no longer a reluctant networker. On the contrary, I now definitely consider myself as an eager networker, a successful connector and a committed enthusiast.

Here's how Noorzaman Rashid, with his strong relator and connector tendencies, networks. He's responsible at Harvey Nash for headhunting executives for board level jobs mainly in central and local government, health and education, and would say that his passion for his charities, plus his own success, plus his understanding of people's business issues are the key to his networking success. How many people do you know who have the names of 3,000 CEOs in their little black book?

....

The man with the little black book

Noorzaman Rashid operates at the highest levels and is an outstanding connector. How come he's so good? His background tells us about what drives his brand of networking.

He was raised with fifteen siblings, the eldest son of the third wife in a mixed Malaysian-Pakistani marriage. His father died when Noorzaman was fifteen and all the children grew up looking after each other, so helping others was deeply ingrained from the outset. There are other drivers, too. He has always hated injustice and is driven to put things right and to help people. As a teenager, when his friends were playing football, thinking about how to get hold of cigarettes, music and girls, he was creating and leading charities.

Success is another driver. For Noorzaman, his own career is of paramount importance: he must succeed himself to be able to help others. By the time he was 27, he was an assistant chief executive responsible for business planning in a £1 billion organisation with over 30,000 people. He has now brought his considerable experience to the headhunting world, with his talent for analysing strategic and tactical problems and mapping out solutions for clients. He builds relationships by spending time with people and looking for ways of helping them; perhaps discussing business issues beyond the assignment or perhaps linking them into networks.

As a result of his charities and his career path, he has built a strong reputation and is known by an estimated 3,000 senior people. He's a prolific communicator and keeps in touch with 1,000 CEOs each month – writing to them about something of interest to them; a dinner here; a congratulatory wish there. He offers his service and becomes their friend. Over good food and wine, he tunes in to what people need, adapting his style: if they're distressed, he listens; if they're strong, he'll challenge; if they're pressed for time, he'll be quick. He's interested to find out about their family and their interests, how they relax after doing such a heavy job. From this, he'll know enough to build and sustain rapport over time.

Noorzaman is out each night of each week with some cost to his personal life. 'You don't work as hard as I do without sacrificing time for my family,' he admits. He still does voluntary work, chairing several committees, and is the co-founder of the Edutrust Foundation which builds new schools in poor areas in Britain. Here, he sits with powerful, influential people and that in turn increases his network – senior people know each other. If they want to reach someone, they can always find the right connections, someone who can make the introductions.

....

Before moving on to other examples, let's take a quick look at what researchers have to say.

Tarzan and Jane: academic research

There's a ton of academic research on the subject of networking and gender. Much is included in Cheryl Travers and Carole Pemberton's *Understanding Networking as a Culturally Differentiated Career Skill*,[3] and here's a tiny taster:

- Researchers agree that networks are most vital when people value them without expecting benefits. (Sonnenberg, 1990)[5]

- Networking is both behaviour and skill. The strength of the ties will be determined by amount of time, emotional intensity and mutual confiding and reciprocal services that characterise the tie. (Granovetter, 1973)[6]

- Strength of tie is characterised by frequency of contact, level of closeness and degree of reciprocity between individuals. (Marsden, 1990)[7]

- Research has suggested that men include more co-workers in their networks than women. (Fischer and Oliker)[8]

- Using networks to share information with others, women empower themselves and gain support and respect from others. (Segerman-Peck, 1991)[9]

It all adds up to the same message: people have many different reasons for and different ways of connecting with others and use their networks for many different reasons. Here's another example. For several years, I've worked with a brilliant networker, Mark Daldorf, who is senior vice-president, organisation learning and talent management, at Standard Chartered First Bank in South Korea. He has lots of woo characteristics and calls his art 'seductive schmoozing'. Just by being funny and friendly and chatting to anyone, anywhere, he has serendipitously built an enormous circle of different sorts of people and generously introduces people to each other across countries and continents for all sorts of reasons, often completely unrelated to business. If you want to find out where to buy a rug in Dubai, Mark's the man to talk to.

Mark has lived in six different countries in Europe, South-east Asia, North-east Asia and the Middle East so he has a wide-reaching network of contacts. How did he get to be such a good connector? In his first ten years of schooling, he went to thirteen schools in two different countries. He had to develop social skills quickly or face peer rejection, and that was the genesis of his great networking. He reckons he helps people far more than he is helped, and that's fine by him. He makes a point of remembering some detail about each person to build rapport; he'll never miss the opportunity of reminding me of some woe that has befallen Arsenal whenever he and I speak.

You can't replicate Mark's style or his background. But you can borrow snippets from here and there that will help you and will fit well with your way of doing things. Helping people, even with non-work things, and remembering things about them are two particularly good things to borrow from him.

To borrow one of Jack Welch's favourite metaphors: networks are a bit like gardens; if you tend them frequently, they'll flourish.

Adam Oliver, of BT, has tended his flourishing network in his own inimitable style. He is the definitive 'coffee shop communicator': he embraces random characters that come into his life and meets informally, preferring Starbucks as his office to a BT meeting room. 'I collect nice people,' he declares. He keeps a nice people list, more a 'who's nice' than a 'who's who' list, which he adds to daily. He just knows who the nice people are; it's all in their tone of voice, their style, their demeanour and aura. Out of the 100,000 people at BT, these nice people are his matrix of 'go to' people – good communicators, good at what they do. He connects them together and gets them talking to each other across the organisation.

'Random lines stitch us together.' Through this matrix he can make things happen. 'I surround myself with good people and together we do stuff that people ask for. So I become a yes person, the go to person who knows where to go for help. Everything is based on who you know and knowing who to speak to. One telephone call to the right person is often enough to resolve a complicated issue.'

How does he meet new people? He talks about random encounters a lot. He just susses out who's interesting and approachable and gets talking to them. He gave me an example as an illustration. He was in a lift in BT Centre when he saw someone scrolling on a BlackBerry (and it was Adam's influence that brought BlackBerries into BT). 'Hey, there's an easier way to do that – you can just press a space bar.' Then they got talking, finding out who did what, and bingo, another nice person is added to the list.

Networking, then, is not just about collecting contacts like trophies. It's not about bothering, pestering or using people. It's not about being pushy and it's not a contest to see who can collect the most business cards, or shake the most hands. It is about quality connections, meaningful relationships and building a reputation based on personal style, as Gill Bruce of Coutts has done.

The intrepid adventurer

If there's a mountain to climb, or a tricky trail to follow, you'll find Gill there raising money for her favourite charity. So far she's tackled the Inca trail in Peru, Everest, Cotopaxi in Ecuador, Kilimanjaro and the Great Wall of China. She is known throughout Coutts for her fundraising adventures, and they have raised her profile across the organisation.

Networking is an essential part of her job and she is a genuine connector, genuinely interested in people, genuinely passionate about her job and always keen to move the agenda forward. She notices where people aren't connecting, where they need to talk, and she'll put them together, making both practical and strategic connections. She's always been curious about people, curious about their jobs, so by listening and learning she finds it easy to identify who should talk to whom. She is warm and witty and uses her Scottish humour to get things done. It flows through her e-mails and peppers her conversations, making her engaging and fun to be around.

Joining RBS from local government as a diversity manager at the age of 31 was another adventure and a shock to her public sector system. She found herself in a foreign world, not knowing a soul, and was completely lost. She puts her disorientation down to the fact that she had no network. So she got herself a buddy and began creating a new network, the key to integration in her new world. 'You have to know people: you have to know where to go, whom to ask, how to get things done,' says Gill. As her internal network grew she was exposed to opportunities within the group, and a chance meeting with Sarah Deaves, CEO of Coutts, led her to current role at Coutts in London.

....

Why is networking important?

The rules for work are changing and there is no longer a guarantee of job security. The downsizing and flattening of organisations in the 1980s and 1990s meant that people were out there looking for jobs in ways that they hadn't had to before. Even the previously immune professions and public sector were hit. The concept of a job for life no longer exists; cradle-to-grave careers are a thing of the past, which means that there is a new focus on self-reliance and portfolio careers. In other words, we look out for ourselves and seek jobs and companies that serve our careers best. This has also led to a rising trend of people who opt to work for themselves, including entrepreneurs, contract workers and consultants. Even newly graduated students find it far from automatic that they'll find jobs; it's tough and extremely competitive out there. And, increasingly, jobs and opportunities are found through contacts; anecdotal evidence suggests that this happens 75% of the time.

All of this points to the stark fact that networking skills are essential for survival. Within organisations networking is critical for success, and if you aren't getting seen, you won't get on. It's about being visible and having a reputation, and mastering the gentle art of self-promotion.

How do I stack up?

Here are some questions to help you identify the gaps and strengths of your networking and kick-start your planning:

1 How has my network already served me?
2 Am I connecting with enough people? Is my profile high enough?
3 Who are my professional counterparts, both internal and external?
4 Which outside bodies am I involved with and how useful are they?
5 When talking to people how interested am I in what they're saying?
6 How systematic am I?
7 How often do I try out new ways of networking?
8 How rigorous am I about following up?
9 How often do I remember to let people know how their introduction has worked out?
10 How daring or cautious am I in approaching people I don't know?
11 How informed am I about what's going on in my sector?
12 How far is this true of me: I'm a good conversationalist and people enjoy talking to me?

What conclusions do you draw about your own connecting skills as you answered the questions, and what should you do next?

The next section shows the lessons to be learned from the role models so you can decide what will make the most difference to you.

What do I do?

Knowing who you are is the essential foundation for all networking communication. Knowing yourself ensures that you can convey to others what you're all about, what you're looking for and what you have to offer. So having completed the first three themes of the blueprint, you're well positioned to start taking action. We've taken a look at what networking is and why it's important, so it only remains to answer these questions:

- Who do I network with?
- Where and how can I network so that I enjoy myself?
- When do I network?
- What is the mindset to help me succeed?

Who do I network with?

In an oft-quoted experiment in 1967, Stanley Milgram, a social psychologist, collected the names of 160 unconnected people who lived in Nebraska and mailed them each a packet. In the packet was the name and address of a stockbroker who worked in Boston. Each was asked to write their name on the packet and forward it to someone they thought would be more closely connected to the stockbroker. Astonishingly, Milgram found that most of the packages came back to the stockbroker having gone through only five or six people. It is this experiment that has given rise to the concept of the six degrees of separation. It concluded that most of us are linked to the world through a few special 'connectors', individuals

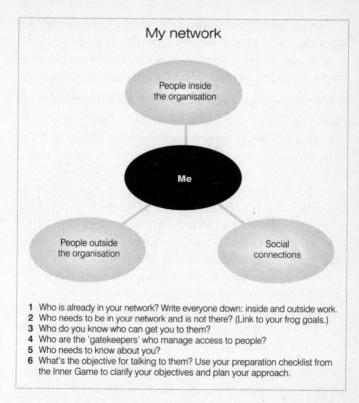

My network

People inside
the organisation

Me

People outside
the organisation

Social
connections

1 Who is already in your network? Write everyone down: inside and outside work.
2 Who needs to be in your network and is not there? (Link to your frog goals.)
3 Who do you know who can get you to them?
4 Who are the 'gatekeepers' who manage access to people?
5 Who needs to know about you?
6 What's the objective for talking to them? Use your preparation checklist from
the Inner Game to clarify your objectives and plan your approach.

who seem to know a huge number of other people. The art of successful networking is being a connector or knowing one.

We test this theory at seminars and it almost always works. We choose someone unlikely to be on anyone's Christmas list, say Richard Branson, Tony Blair, Madonna, Nelson Mandela or Bill Gates. Asking the question 'who knows anyone who might lead us to this person?' we invariably find someone who knows someone who can get us there, often in fewer than six degrees. We all know upward of 250 people.[10] If each of these also knows upward of 250 people, your six degrees starts with upward of 62,500. You've got to be impressed with that. So let's start by looking at whom you know (see figure).

The measure of someone's competency today is not only knowing a lot but also knowing people who know things. A large and broad network doesn't guarantee success, but without one it is far more difficult to succeed.

Where and how can I network so that I enjoy myself?
Daniel Goleman, in his new book, *Social Intelligence*,[11] says that we are wired to connect and social intelligence is the term he uses to describe where and how we connect with each other. There is an infinite wealth of ideas and approaches about how to do this, and beyond these there are still more. Good networkers develop their social intelligence and keep going beyond what's expected. New technology now drives how people network. E-mail, websites and blogging mean that networking is fundamentally different today; it's much more about sharing and exchanging information whether you're in Melbourne, Milan or Manchester.

Way beyond the concept of 'working a room' there are at least 101 other places and ways to connect with people. In the context of networking, start by asking yourself:

- What are my interests and passions?
- What do I enjoy doing and what am I good at?

In my experience, people then come up with a creative array of options that suit them down to the ground and energise them. Here are some examples from people I am currently working with:

- 'I like to be a thought leader, so I write articles for the trade press and I run seminars to keep people informed. I meet so many people and so many doors are now open to me. People actually approach me now because I've built a reputation. It doesn't feel like hard work.' (private banker)

- 'I am mad about rugby and wine. Although I consider myself to be quite an introvert, I find it easy to build relationships with people around these twin passions. I'm always letting people know about related events that I come across and inviting people to join me has enlarged my circle in a way I like. The people I know invite people they know. Taking the step to talk business is a small one. I wish I'd done this earlier.' (business development director)

- 'I am most comfortable building a strong relationship based on trust and respect. I always keep in touch with people and we meet, informally and regularly. We introduce people to each other, over a coffee or a good meal. I'm most comfortable with this way of networking and it has reaped rewards in terms of business leads both ways.' (operations manager)

- 'I work extensively for charities that are close to my heart which I find personally rewarding. In addition, I get the positive benefits of raising my profile and I meet a wide range of senior people from many organisations. It's easy to build good business relationships this way, too.' (managing director)

- 'I consider myself a crazy, fun-loving extrovert and I love to party. So I create events with wacky themes, which are always huge fun, and I invite clients and suppliers to these. Everyone knows who I am. People take the call from me when I phone.' (recruitment manager)

What follows is a cornucopia of ideas, garnered from everywhere, for you to try out, whether you're looking for a new job, seeking new ideas or raising your profile.

....

Networking ideas

Meeting people

- Trade shows
- Conferences and conventions
- Careers fairs
- Training courses
- Networking groups
- Online networks
- Blogs
- Evening classes
- At the gym
- Fundraising
- In a lift
- On a plane
- At the theatre

Raising your profile

- Prepare weekly update reports highlighting your results and those of your team
- Share best practice
- Go to high-profile conferences and report back
- Develop a public profile by running seminars on your area of expertise
- Comment regularly on matters in which you want to be seen as an expert
- Get a mentor to open doors for you
- Be a mentor
- Comment on blogs
- Have your own blog
- Get published in the company newsletter
- Volunteer for projects
- Get involved in what's going on in your organisation: eg, sports, charity, social
- Be a buddy
- Use your PR company to get into the media
- Write a book or research paper

- Voice your ideas at meetings
- Grab opportunities to make presentations
- Ask yourself: what can I do to help others? Who would value my skills and knowledge?
- Send carefully selected, relevant and valuable information to people
- Introduce people to others

....

When do I network?

Networking happens all the time, anywhere and everywhere. It can be as impromptu as a random conversation with the person sitting next to you on a plane; meeting someone on a training programme; or an introduction from your cousin to someone who knows someone. I call it the serendipity factor; chance meetings that lead to chance opportunities. It's worked for David Gold, CEO of ProspectUs:

> Serendipity led me to the not-for-profit sector and I
> learned my craft with an organisation forging links
> between business and the community. Again serendipity
> led me to discover a small business for sale which would
> enable me to build capacity in the not-for-profit sector.
> Luck has played an important role in my career.

Your network is about relationships, to be nurtured and enjoyed for their own sake without keeping score or necessarily expecting a return. It then becomes entirely natural to turn to people for help without feeling that you're using them. People are invariably only too willing to help. Don't wait until you know that your current job is about to end before getting out your little black book. You'll be more enthused and less desperate if you're already employed in a meaty job.

People do, however, use their networks specifically when looking for a job. Lisa Fabian Lustigman of Withers has always made sure of a good, solid network of contacts:

When I was ready to move, I put my name out there. In my crazy paving career, two out of my three significant legal jobs developed from personal contacts. The first came out of a personal relationship, the second from a colleague from a different firm. Having the introduction is absolutely no guarantee of a job, you still need to be Bloody Good, but it's a jolly good start.

And people turn to their networks when they need support, as Trisha Watson, of Microsoft, reveals:

I came through my difficult time with my boss by talking to my close network of friends and colleagues, whom I call my trusted advisers. This helped me to get another view on things; the people who know you well can help you to know yourself and to restore a sense of confidence and perspective.

What is the mindset to help me succeed?

The more I talk to people, the more it appears that, whatever the individual networking style, eight principles sit at the heart of what successful networkers have. These are: abundance, curiosity, enthusiasm, discipline, integrity, reciprocity, learning and communication.

1 Abundance

People with this mindset don't fear how they'll lose out by giving; they are confident that there's plenty for everyone. They are inclusive and bring people together. They tend to be proud of making things happen for others, rather than about the number of business cards they've collected. They work out how they can help others, rather than focusing on what others can do for them.

If you've been on the receiving end of this generosity, you'll know how wonderful it feels.

Ask yourself:

● How abundant is my mindset? How generous am I?

- What can I do to help others?
- Who specifically can I help?
- When will I make the opportunity?

Then get into action.

2 Curiosity

I always remember the words of my Year 12 English teacher, Miss Hutchinson: 'To be bored is to be boring.' She was right, and it's true that the responsibility for being interested and curious rests with us; it's not up to someone else to be interesting for us.

People with a mindset of curiosity can engage in conversation with almost anyone because they feel that there is always something to learn; they are genuinely curious to find out more. I recently met Andrew Haigh, head of strategic projects, marketing, at Coutts. He is someone who really enjoys networking and is good at it. He has a mindset of curiosity and is genuinely energised by people. So when Andrew asks you questions, he really listens to the answers, learns from you and knows what will help you. He takes the long-term view and his network, based firmly on the principles of reciprocity, has been built steadily over a 20-year period. 'Leave your ego behind and focus on others when they speak,' is his advice.

Ask yourself:

- What am I really thinking about when people are speaking to me?
- What am I naturally curious about?
- How specifically do I listen and communicate when I'm naturally curious?

Becoming aware of your thoughts and responses will help you to focus. One way to still the self-talk that stops us listening is to wonder about things. 'I wonder' will develop the habit of being curious – I wonder how; I wonder what; I wonder who. 'I wonder' is a good pebble in the murky waters of ennui. And it may follow that to be interested is to be interesting.

3 Enthusiasm

People with this mindset enjoy themselves and find pleasure sharing their passions with others. Others want to be around them and find them energising. Enthusiasm and passion are infectious and make engaging with you fun, energising, inspiring and memorable.

Ask yourself:

- What do I enjoy doing?
- What stimulates me?
- What am I passionate about?

Build this into your relationships with others, allowing it to influence where you meet and what you talk about. A word of caution: one man's (or woman's) enthusiasm is another's insult. Be culturally aware, in rapport and appropriate. Talking about sex, politics and religion is rarely a good idea. Neither is circulating political diatribes or chain e-mails, however noble or hilarious the cause.

4 Discipline

I was once told the probably apocryphal story of Elton John and the pillows. The story goes that Elton John arrived at his hotel, was welcomed with enthusiasm and shown to his room. He settled in, unpacked and went to bed. But he couldn't settle. He wasn't quite comfortable enough and just couldn't fall asleep, so he called the housekeeper and asked for a couple more pillows. They were delivered, were just what he needed, and he was so comfortable that he fell asleep immediately. It just so happened that some years later, he was in the same area and coincidentally checked into the very same hotel. He was welcomed with enthusiasm and shown to his room. He settled in and while he was unpacking, there was a knock at the door. When he opened it, there was a housekeeper: 'Good evening, Sir Elton, welcome to the hotel. Here are your extra pillows.'

Such a stand-out 'wow' service is not based on good memory; it's based on discipline and systems. Disciplined networkers use the plethora of useful tools around to help: Microsoft Outlook calendar and contacts, personal organisers, lists and time-planning systems all work well. Those of us who can't count on brilliant memories daily bless our pop-up reminders. Disciplined networkers always make a point of follow-up, so often the stage missed out of networking. Like the hotel, they keep a note of who they've met, where they met them, what they promised to do for them and when to get in touch again. They record unusual bits of information and use these in fresh ways that make them stand out.

Ask yourself:

- What systems am I currently using?
- What is working well?
- What is slipping through the net?
- How can technology help me?
- What do I need to stop, start, continue?

Then get into action.

5 Integrity

People with this mindset keep their word and deliver on their promises. They respect people and remember the courtesies.

There are unwritten rules about the dos and don'ts that govern what is acceptable behaviour. Ignoring them is common, but it damages trust. I once went to a talk given by a networking guru. 'Respond to e-mails,' he informed us. 'Introductions are sacred: thank people; let them know what's happening; let them know the outcome; see how you can help them in return.' Enthused, I introduced him to someone;

they met; and he got a juicy piece of work as a result. Unfortunately, I never heard from him again and it was more a case of do as I say, not as I do: no reply, no thanks, no follow-through. Integrity is not just a matter of saying the right things; it's about being true to your word, doing what you say and about keeping confidences; it's about courtesy and respect – and all of these build solid trust and credibility over time.

Ask yourself:

- How do I make sure I follow up?
- Who do I need to update or thank right now?
- Where am I acting without integrity?
- How will I repair the damage?

6 Reciprocity

A man I knew was once between jobs and got in touch with me. We agreed to meet for tea at the Institute of Directors. I just couldn't figure out any way that I would be of help to him and was on the brink of cancelling, even though tea would have been pleasant. But I went ahead based on the philosophy that 'it's always worth it; you never know how things might turn out'. As it happened, when he told me what he was looking for, I realised that I knew a CEO in his exact target sector. I introduced them, not certain whether there would be any mutual interest. What came out of this chance meeting? The CEO happened to be looking for someone with his skill set and he ended up with a job; it was a wonderful opportunity for him. The delighted CEO called to thank me and we met for a glass (or two) of mellow merlot. In catching up with each other, we discovered areas of current mutual interest and he became a major client, someone I always love working with.

It doesn't end there. The man-with-a-new-job also phoned to thank me and in turn introduced me to someone who introduced me to someone who became a new client. All this came from a simple favour and a cup of tea. Reciprocity works like that. People with this mindset take a view that what goes around comes around and do not seek direct or immediate payback.

Jeff Grout, a business consultant and author, is a generous and abundant connector. His networking is based on reciprocity, or in his words being an 'old hippy': help others and ultimately you help yourself because in networking you get back what you give, though not in a tit-for-tat way. A word of caution, though: there is a balance to be struck. If you find that you are making all the effort with someone and it is clearly not being reciprocated, then back off and tread water with the relationship.

Approach your networking with a mindset of 'I wonder'. 'I wonder where this will lead. I wonder how this will work out. I wonder how we'll help each other.' This mindset is about relaxing expectations and going with the flow.

Act as if you believe that 'what goes around comes around' and that the return favours will come from somewhere, sometime. What's different? What does that feel like?

7 Learning

People with this mindset are current in their knowledge, widely read and aware of what's going on in the world. Albert Ellis, CEO of Harvey Nash, has some cutting-edge advice from his vantage point in the headhunting world. He sees so many people being distinctly average when seeking jobs. He too stresses the importance of having a good network:

> People get their dream jobs not only through an
> exclusive relationship with a single headhunter, but also
> through internal promotions, their own networks and
> casting their net as widely as possible. In conversations,
> whether networking or when being interviewed, too
> many people have only the most basic knowledge
> of the organisation and sector. You need to connect
> with people: do you have mutual contacts, are there

experiences in common? You must do your research;
it's not enough to look at the website and quote the
annual report. That's distinctly ordinary and off-putting.
Understand their strategic issues, know their PR issues;
be familiar with what people are saying about them
– whether it's someone in their local community or a
disgruntled employee mouthing off on a personal blog.

It's crucial to stay informed, essential to be up to speed
with the comings and goings in your chosen industries. This
will help you spot potential opportunities for others in your
network and build your reputation as someone who is up
to date. This also applies to what's going on in your current
organisation and sector for internal networking; become a
massive sponge for absorbing information.

Here are some of the ways that people stay clued up:

- Read tabloids and broadsheets
- Read trade papers
- Scan websites
- Review blogs
- Scavenge the internet
- Talk to people and listen to what they tell you
- Subscribe to the *Harvard Business Review*, *Hoovers* and *The Economist*
- Go to lectures
- Go on training courses
- Attend industry conferences
- Read business books
- Know about the competition
- Watch news programmes
- Listen to radio debates
- Listen to informative tapes and CDs

Which come naturally to you? Which fit in with your preferred way of learning? What specifically will you do? And when?

Hippy groups are a great way to keep this alive. Some groups allocate topics and then brief each other at one of their meetings. This means that it gets done, you learn from each other and you save time.

8 Communication

I once went to a networking seminar where the speaker gave us a task. She asked us to hook up with someone in the room we didn't already know, or at least didn't know well. Then she gave us two or three minutes to have a conversation. The objective of the exercise was to find a person we knew in common. We were astonished at the number of connections we all managed to make. And because we'd been focused on the task, we all had entirely natural conversations without resorting to ready-prepared introductions, well-rehearsed anecdotes or calculated questions. Try it out for yourself. This simple exercise taught me to use and offer advice on conversations with great caution because the most effective conversations are when we're natural, authentic and 'in the flow'. Having said that, here are some hints, tips and guidelines for you to unpack and check out for conversations with impact, elevator speeches, working a room and presentations, with a tiny word about bios and CVs.

Conversations with impact

Networking involves selling yourself and this shouldn't be something to shy away from. According to TACK International, sales training specialists, sales skills are social skills: good selling is primarily about asking open questions, showing an interest in the other person by actively listening to their answers and showing respect. Sound familiar? Absolutely everything we've looked at before will apply here too, so here's a quick reminder:

- Act 'as if' you're confident and relaxed.
- Adopt your grounded physiology and good posture.
- Build rapport by tuning in to others and matching their style.
- Have empathy by entering their world.
- Use positive, fresh language; use metaphors and anecdotes.
- Apply the basics – show respect; share ideas; listen and ask questions; follow up.

Let's take a further look at some of the skills that apply specifically in the context of networking.

Dos and don'ts of conversation

1 Do use stories and anecdotes to hook people's interest. Andrew Haigh of Coutts believes that just by having engaging conversations you are able to make an immediate impact and be memorable. He will pepper his conversations with anecdotes that pique interest and are remembered. For example, at the time of the World Cup, instead of bringing up the usual 'did you see that game?' he found a lesser known and interesting fact he'd heard on the *Today* programme on Radio Four: 'Did you know that just two national flags on a car add £1 per week to the running costs? The environmental cost of patriotism!'

2 Do ask questions, but don't interrogate; do listen but also share your own views. This should give you ample opportunity to spot mutual interests and build rapport. People who are good communicators strike a good balance between listening and speaking in conversation. Don't work to a formula; instead, dance freely in the conversation. It's best to be natural and be yourself.

3 Do find a natural way to get a conversation started if you're meeting someone for the first time. Sometimes you'll choose the simplest of approaches: How do you know so and so? Have you come far? How was the traffic? Where are you based? Oscar Wilde may be right that 'conversation about the weather is the last refuge of the unimaginative', but in Britain it's a staple and comfortable opening gambit. You may choose to use a story or current event to open with, so scan your favourite tabloid or broadsheet for hot gossip or weighty comment.

4 Do use appropriate social behaviour; there's no 'off duty' when networking and business codes of conduct apply. Be careful with drink, jokes and flirting, and be clear about who pays for what, making sure that you take your turn.

5 Do use people's names.

6 Do use eye contact but don't stare.

Elevator speech

If you bumped into the chief executive of the company going up in a lift, and you had around the 30 seconds it takes from the ground floor to her floor, how would you introduce yourself with panache? Your 30-second message is what is known as an elevator speech. As a businessperson introducing yourself to a prospective client, you must establish both rapport and credibility within your 30 seconds, or you will be dismissed as just more marketing noise. During any conversation, however many questions you ask, however much listening you do, at some point you are going to have to talk about yourself: who you are, what you do, what you stand for. When asked what we do, too many of us splutter something garbled and under-whelming, like: 'I, er, well, I sort of do some … help out with marketing projects for Major Corp.'

Dos and don'ts of elevator speeches

1 Do present yourself in best possible light but don't
   embellish the truth so much that you are misleading.
   Some Tarzans brag or are pushy and that's off-putting for
   most people. Janes, however, have a natural tendency to
   undersell themselves and talk about weaknesses. So what
   Tarzans and Janes should be aiming for is the happy
   balance of not broadcasting your failures or bragging
   about your success.

2 Do use people you have in common to help the other
   person continue the conversation and build a connection
   – 'I'm Jane Smith. I worked with Joe Jones on the merger'
   or 'Joe Jones told me about your success with the product
   development pipeline.' A sincere compliment won't go
   amiss.

3 Don't be obvious; introduce yourself with panache.
   People are invariably so literal when describing what
   they do. 'I work in the finance department of Major Corp
   and I'm responsible for the management accounting.'
   There's nothing wrong with that; it just doesn't say
   anything about you, it's not memorable, and you won't
   stand out. I'll always remember the way a private banker
   introduced herself: 'I help all sorts of people sort out
   their money; it may be a pig farmer from Leicestershire
   or a Lord from Berkshire. It's hugely interesting and I
   love what I do!'

4 Don't use set scripts. The elevator is already too full of
   pre-packaged conversations, which come across as glib
   and insincere; they do not build rapport. Think beyond
   the elevator and focus on the other person. One of my
   clients told me about a presentation he'd been to, given
   by a well-known speaker. Afterwards, there was the usual
   milling around when he noticed that the speaker looked
   tired and was still surrounded by people. He got a drink,

went up to her and said, 'It looks as if you could do with
this.' She was grateful. They got talking. She remembered
him.

5   Don't be self-conscious; you don't have to be perfect.
Contrary to what is often taught, you don't have to
worry endlessly about ums and ers. This is true if you
build rapport, are comfortable and confident, and have
all the basics we've talked about in place. Just listen
to people. Tony Blair uses the 'er' word quite a lot and
he is very skilled when it comes to communicating his
message powerfully. Hardly shrinking violets, Richard
Branson and Michael Parkinson both 'um'. And after his
stroke, when his language was far from what it used to
be, Kirk Douglas gave powerfully engaging interviews. So
relax and enjoy the conversation.

Working a room

We began this theme by listing all the reasons people avoid
networking based on the assumption that it's about working
a room. But though a lot of people hate it, some people love
it and are really good at it. I know one or two people who are
brilliant at it. One particular person comes to mind, Clive
Sexton of Impact Executives, a man of great charm. He told
me how systematically he approaches his brand of networking and about all that he does before, during and after an
event. This is his advice.

Dos and don'ts of working a room

1 Do prepare your mindset; be aware that others might be
feeling conspicuous and nervous. Replace any negative
feelings you have with positive thoughts and anchors.

2 Do look at the guest list in advance and identify who you
want to meet.

3 Do research on the individuals you want to meet.

4 Do research their organisations.

5 Do research their marketplace.

6 Do research what key players in their sector are doing.

7 Do arrange to be introduced.

8 Do size up the room; do a couple of circuits before approaching someone.

9 Don't go for large groups; it's easier to approach someone on their own.

10 Do make for the food and drink; it's easy to get talking over a sausage roll.

11 Don't skulk in a corner pretending to read.

12 Do state your name slowly; events can be noisy and you want them to remember you; and do use their name in conversation.

13 Do face the door so you can see who's coming in; and stand by the door when people are beginning to leave as they're usually more relaxed by this stage so it's easier to open a conversation.

14 Do use eye contact and avoid looking around while people are talking to you.

15 Do use positive, strong, clear language and good body language.

16 Do seek permission to contact them again.

17 Do find a valid business reason to call the person after the event and do follow up rigorously.

I was on the receiving end of his rigorous follow-up recently and I was impressed. I bumped into Clive in the street once on my way to a meeting. We had a quick chat about what we'd both been up to and as a result, he promised to send me a link to a business forum, something I was interested in. By the time I returned to my office, less than an hour later, the e-mail with the link was already there. And he remembered to ask me about it the next time we met. He now gives me feedback from sessions I've not been able to attend.

Presentations

Public speaking or presenting is a great way to build reputation. It gives an opportunity to provide thought leadership that positions you as an authority on your subject and to reach large numbers of people who'll get to know you and what you do. However, presentations terrify many people and doing them well takes more than the advice of actor and playwright Noel Coward: 'Just say the lines and don't trip over the furniture.'

Dos and don'ts of presenting

1 Do your homework: every audience requires a different approach. In preparing, ask: who are they and what's my message? What do I want them to remember? What do I want them to feel? What do they want to hear, rather than what I want to say?

2 Do prepare so you are confident, fluent and articulate. Think ahead to what 'killer questions' might come up, the questions you dread the most, and then prepare how you'd answer them. Don't read your presentation; speak it. Do use small note cards with bullets or mind maps to prompt you. Don't stand up clutching reams of A4 paper covered with your text or people will switch off immediately.

3 Do use a structure. I was trained an eternity ago to 'tell them what you'll tell them; tell them; tell them what you told them'. Not a bad summary. There are so many formulae, but this remains my favourite way to structure a presentation.

4 Do find a 'hook' to start with. Perhaps a question that whets the appetite: 'Did you know that around

1.3 billion Coca-Cola beverage servings are sold each day?' Perhaps a dramatic statement: 'Fewer than 1% of board directors are women.' Or there's the technique that comedians use when telling a story. They start as if they're in the middle of a conversation. 'So I said to her…' or 'There I was …'

5 Do stick to a few key points rather than cover everything. People take in and remember remarkably little of what you say. Use pictures and tell stories to make your message more memorable. Use all the pointers on powerful language that we looked at in Be Bloody Good and Turn Up The Volume.

6 Do watch as many presentations as you can find. Look at the greats in action and learn by modelling yourself on them. I like to search the websites of speaker bureaux and look at video clips of their top speakers.

7 Do use the 'as if' mindset and affirming self-talk to manage your state and feel confident. There are plenty of other 'as if' resourceful states, such as calm, excited and powerful. Visualise yourself up there doing a great job.

8 Do find ways of establishing your brand, from logos and colours to music and room settings.

9 Do occupy the space available. Don't stand like a rabbit rooted to the spot. Use large and expansive body language. Watch actors on stage and notice their movements. Acting classes will improve your stage presence.

10 Do stick to your time. Less is more, and, as Mark Twain said, 'Few sinners are saved after the first 20 minutes of a sermon.'

Adam Oliver of BT believes that your message must have an emotive impact and encourages people not to be afraid to show emotions. 'Tarzans, get in touch with your inner Jane,' he urges.

A final word about bios and CVs

However modest and understated you choose to be in your face-to-face conversations, your written message is a marketing document designed to open doors for you and to sell you to the reader. It must be punchy, confident, sophisticated, delivery focused and extremely well crafted. Highlight your most significant achievements. Use references and third-party testimonials to back up your claims and enhance your credibility. Do match your style to your target audience.

Don't Just Sit There: conclusion

You can now get out there and be seen and known – without manipulating a single soul. You've discovered the way you connect best, in your own style, and answered all the questions about who, when, where and how. With the eight principles behind you, you're all set to build a thriving community of enthusiastic people who will help you as you help them.

What do I do now?

Once again, as you went through the exercises and read about the role models, as you took cashmere-socks moments of reflective thinking, you will have absorbed and integrated some of your insights already so you need take no further action on those.

- Reread the Making it Stick section at the beginning of the book (page xxii); the suggestions apply equally to all the themes and will show you what to do step-by-step.

- If you are curious to learn more, take a look at the What if I want to do more? section at the back (page 188) for resources to help you on your way.

- Get started!

The Leader's Part

With this book as a guide providing insights, hints and tips, Tarzans and Janes can take charge of their own careers. They can look within and edit what's there; define what they want and what's important to them; build self-confidence; and by honing and enhancing their signature strengths they can build on their natural talents to create a natural and aligned brand. This is what they take to the outside world when building a network of supportive relationships, and this is what will have them thriving in the corporate jungle.

Although the emphasis has been on the need for individuals to take responsibility, surely others should take responsibility too. What about the employer's share of the responsibility for improving the corporate jungle and for helping Tarzans and Janes on their way? Surely organisations and their leaders must play a huge part. In a world where knowledge and customer service are so highly prized, where the individual is 'king' and has choice, companies will face a huge challenge if they do not attract or engage employees. It's not a given that people will want to work for you. You have to compete for talented people in a diverse labour market that is not what it was. You have to adapt to the needs of this new market and recognise that employees want different things. For a start, given the scope of this book, you need to appeal to both 'new' men and 'new' women. In appealing to them, it's important to acknowledge how the context for their work is different from what it was. Demographics, the pace of change, globalisation, regulation, competition and technology all add up to long working hours and make the jobs challenging in a way that would have been unimaginable just a few years ago. Add shareholder pressure to the mix and you begin to see why life in the 21st century corporate jungle is so complex.

There are social changes, too. Many families now have two working parents and men are increasingly sharing the responsibilities of parenting as they too seek more flexible working patterns. Many men tell me that they are no longer prepared to work in the stressful '24/7' way that so many companies require of their people.

Then there's the sheer volume of women to empower and engage. Women constitute 41% of the European workforce and yet occupy only 10% of management positions and make up a mere 1% of board members.[1] The same pattern is evident all over the world.[2] We tend to observe that this reflects unfairness and discrimination, which it undoubtedly does. But it also lacks logic. Organisations are missing out on half their intellectual capacity and leadership potential.

So it's smart business sense and logic rather than political correctness or anything soft and fluffy that is driving enlightened leaders to work at being inclusive and making their companies more appealing places to work. They are seeking more flexible and innovative approaches to help them attract and retain the talented people who will give them their competitive edge.

As an example, Sarah Deaves, CEO of Coutts, is doing significant things to make life better at Coutts, such as:

- introducing flexible work options
- ensuring that senior women have visibility

- providing careers coaching and mentoring for men and women
- creating an environment where both men and women can work together successfully.

It's clear that there is an array of creative options to choose from depending on your business, your budget and your aims, but unless there is also a change in organisational culture and in people's attitudes, your initiatives will be merely decorative. The biggest responsibility for change rests with leaders, and a good place to start is with leadership style. In the new corporate jungle the transactional, 'command and control' style of leadership, usually but not exclusively attributed to men, is failing companies. According to research, leaders who fail are often impatient, manipulative, dominating, self-important and critical of others. These 'Rambos in pinstripes'[3] neglect teamwork and lack the ability to develop talent in others. This style of leadership is also known to create stress, which costs the UK an estimated £6.4 billion a year.[4] What works better is the transformational, motivational and supportive style of leadership, usually but not exclusively attributed to women, which engages, empowers and creates high morale. A more authentic leadership style is what people are telling us they value in survey after survey. For people to be engaged they need to trust their leaders. Trust is only earned gradually over a period of time and is built on all the elements of the authentic personal brand we have been looking at throughout this book.

Leaders, you need to be in charge of this agenda and drive it from the top; you need to pay attention to it and not just sit there; you must show by your behaviour that it's important. Listening to people, enabling them to Turn Up The Volume, and focusing on how to help them to realise their potential, is what good leaders are already doing. Creating a culture of trust, respect, empowerment and high performance will unleash potential and drive productivity. It will make sure that you're being Bloody Good and that people will choose you; they'll give you their commitment and loyalty, their time, their energy and their passion, so that you, too, can thrive in the new corporate jungle.

How does your organisation stack up?

- What's the attrition rate of your high potentials?
- What percentage of these is high performing women?
- What percentage of these is under 30?
- How prevalent are 'Rambos in pinstripes'?
- How well do your leaders score for transformational leadership and emotional intelligence?
- How diverse is your senior leadership team?
- What is your reputation in the labour market: are you attracting the best?
- What innovative approaches do you offer: flexible working, job share, home working?
- How productive are the stress levels in your organisation?
- What are your absence levels like and what impact do they have on productivity?
- Do you measure employee engagement?
- What do your employees have to say about you, and are Tarzans and Janes of all ages thriving?
- What more could you be doing to mine the pool of talent within and to attract people from outside?

Diagnosis and awareness are always the best ways to start, so here's a checklist to kick-start your thinking – it's similar to the process used by individuals.

1 Where are you now? What are the main problems?

2 What is the root cause of the problems?

3 Where do you want to be? What's the gap?

4   Why do you want to get there – what will the business gain? What will this get for you?

5   How and when will you get there? What's the approach? Who needs to be involved? What resources do you already have? What is the effort required relative to the impact? What barriers are in the way?

6   Brainstorm solutions; evaluate and prioritise them. Create SMART+ action plans (Specific, Measurable, Achievable, Realistic, Timed – defined in the positive).

7   How will you define and measure success?

8   Who will be accountable and who will drive the changes?

Like individuals, organisations also need to:

Focus and plan
You can't work on everything right away, so prioritise. What's the most important area for the company to focus on?

Keep it going
It's easy for people to lose focus so you need to keep the vision alive and to put some checks and balances in place.

- First: create a process. Set goals for people and review their progress. Hold yourself and others accountable.
- Second: select a monitoring mechanism to keep projects on track.
- Third: talk about what you're doing at every opportunity, link activities to your vision, reward congruent behaviour and celebrate success.

And finally, get started!

What Next?

What if I want to do more?

If something in this book has piqued your curiosity and you want to know more, there is a world full of resources for you to tap into: people to talk to; books to read; quotes to inspire; experts for advice. This section introduces you to just a sample of what's available.

A word about coaches

If you've identified a need for coaching to accelerate your progress, what follows applies to all of the four themes:

> A coach is someone who tells you what you don't want to hear, who has you see what you don't want to see, so you can be who you have always known you could be.[1]

A personal coach is the way to go for the greatest acceleration. Many organisations now offer coaching as part of a planned development programme, so speak to HR and take advantage of what's on offer. If you're seeking a coach on your own, it's best to get recommendations and meet a few coaches to establish rapport – and do check their credentials. There are too many people who have been on a two-day training programme and set themselves up as coaches. I select highly credible coaches to work with and recommend, people with strong business experience and good insight. I prefer and recommend face-to-face coaching and I prefer people who use a variety of methods.

Recent research identified what people look for when choosing a coach:[2]

- Rapport 87%
- Business experience 74%
- Organisational culture match 49%
- Industry experience 35%
- Recommendation 34%
- Advanced degree 18%
- Accreditation 17%
- Cost 8%

You can take a look at the website of the International Coach Federation, www.coachfederation.com or www.coach-globe.com, where you'll find advice on coaching in general, including how to select a coach, accreditation and ethical issues.

Anchors

Anchors help you to keep the drive alive, they can inspire or soothe. Use pictures, music or quotes to quickly rouse you and remind you what you're up to.

What follows is a sample of books, quotes and websites specific to each of the four themes. Check out www.margot-katz.com for new resources and details of Tarzan and Jane seminars.

The Inner Game

Books

- *The 7 Habits of Highly Effective People*, by Stephen Covey. Free Press, 1989.

A well-known classic oozing pearls of wisdom. A Google search will reveal handy summaries, for example www.businessballs. com.

● *NLP Workbook*, by Joseph O'Connor. HarperCollins, 2001. A practical, user-friendly guide that walks the reader through the helpful techniques and concepts that neuro-linguistic programming has to offer.

● *Embracing Uncertainty*, by Susan Jeffers. Hodder and Stoughton, 2003.
Points out that although we can't control the future, we do have choice. Helps the reader to wonder more and plan less.

● *I'm OK – You're OK*, by Thomas Harris. Pan Books, 1973. Transactional analysis is the study of how people transact using parent, adult and child ego states. It is practical and immediate and offers great tools for self-awareness and communicating effectively with others. Other books on the subject include:

● *Games People Play*, by Eric Berne. Grove Press, 1964;

● *Scripts People Live*, by Claude Steiner. Bantam Psychology Books, 1974;

● *Born to Win*, by Muriel James and Dorothy Jongeward. Addison-Wesley Publishing Company, 1971.

● *Who Moved my Cheese?*, by Dr Spencer Johnson. Vermillion, 1998.
A ten-minute read, an ideal airport book, good for getting you out of your comfort zone.

● *How to Stop Worrying and Start Living*, by Dale Carnegie. Pocket Books, 1944.
This is years old, and perhaps an acquired taste, but it's comforting, and great for worriers. The best-known Dale Carnegie classic is *How to Win Friends and Influence People* (Pocket Books, 1983), which still has relevant hints and tips.

- *Women with Attitude*, by Susan Vinnicombe. Routledge, 2003.

This has thumbnail sketches of nineteen successful women. Good for inspiration.

I also recommend biographies of successful men for inspiration. I've enjoyed: *Losing my Virginity*, by Richard Branson (Crown Business, 1998), and *Jack*, by Jack Welch (Warner Books, 2005), and *Open Secret: The Autobiography of the Former Director-General of MI5*, by Stella Rimington (Hutchinson, 2001).

Courses

Sometimes a book can spark a desire to go deeper and take things further. There is an infinite range of options, but here are three places to explore:

- *Landmark Education*

The Landmark Forum is a great way to blast through your comfort zone and get amazing shifts (www.landmarkeducation.com).

- *Transactional Analysis*

There are some great courses; contact the Institute of Transactional Analysis to find out where to go (www.ita.org.uk).

- *Neuro-Linguistic Programming*

NLP provides a set of tools and techniques that are absolutely brilliant when used in the right hands. As it's not a regulated offering, please do check credentials carefully and make sure you have respect for and rapport with the trainer you use. There are many websites to look at but Robert Dilts, an NLP guru, has a site called the NLP University, which is a mine of information (www.nlpu.com).

Role model websites

David Gold: www.prospect-us.co.uk. And if you'd like to know more about his charities: www.futurebuilders-england.org.uk; www.philanthropyuk.org

Diana Boulter: www.dbaspeakers.com
Roz Savage: www.rozsavage.com

Quotes

I'm a sucker for a good quote and after my seminars it's always my collection of quotes that people want. It is an editor who has stopped me from littering the book with quotes – but this is my moment to indulge.

Here are some Inner Game quotes:

- 'Our aspirations are our possibilities.' Robert Browning
- 'The future belongs to those who believe in the beauty of their dreams.' Eleanor Roosevelt
- 'Do what you can, with what you have, where you are.' Theodore Roosevelt
- 'Do not wait for leaders; do it alone, person to person.' Mother Teresa
- 'If I am not for myself, who will be for me? If am only for myself, what am I? And if not now, when?' Rabbi Hillel
- 'Nothing will ever be attempted if all possible objections must be first overcome.' Samuel Johnson
- 'The unexamined life is not worth living.' Socrates
- 'Above all things never think that you're not good enough yourself. My belief is that in life people will take you very much at your own reckoning.' Anthony Trollope
- 'No one can make you feel inferior without your consent.' Eleanor Roosevelt
- 'There is nothing either good or bad, but thinking makes it so.' Shakespeare's *Hamlet*
- 'Our greatest honour is not in never failing, but in rising every time we fail.' Confucius
- 'Leap and the net will appear.' Sahar Hashemi

- 'Life is a field of unlimited possibilities.' Deepak Chopra
- 'Keep away from people who try to belittle your ambitions – small people always do that; but the really great make you feel that you, too, can somehow become great.' Mark Twain
- 'It is easy to criticise and break down the spirit of others, but to know yourself takes a lifetime.' Bruce Lee
- 'Too much of a good thing can be wonderful.' Mae West (This is especially good for those of us who don't believe we deserve too much and who need 'permission' for good things to happen.)

Be Bloody Good

Books

- *The 7 Habits of Highly Effective People*, by Stephen Covey. Free Press, 1989.

The sharp saw concept is particularly worth reading

- *Now, Discover Your Strengths*, by Marcus Buckingham and Donald O. Clifton. Simon & Schuster, 2002.

This practical and readable book takes a fresh look at how to develop your talents and those of the people you manage. With each book is a code that allows you to take their test at www.strengthfinder.com.

- *Good to Great*, by Jim Collins. Random House Business Books, 2001.

One of the best business books, a 'must read'. Many of the lessons for companies are applicable to individuals, too. Level 5 Leadership is a particularly important chapter to read.

- 'Why should anyone be led by you?', by Robert Goffee and Gareth Jones. *Harvard Business Review*, October 2000.

Asks challenging questions and highlights top ways for leaders to build trust.

● *The Dilbert Principle*, by Scott Adams. HarperCollins, 1996.
A great reminder of how ridiculous the world of work can
be and how not to get caught up in nonsensical polices and
procedures in our search for Bloody Good solutions.

● *Working with Emotional Intelligence*, by Daniel Goleman.
  Bloomsbury Publishing, 1998.
Daniel Goleman is the definitive authority on the subject of
EQ and has written many books on the subject since 1995. This
happens to be the one I refer to most. Margaret Chapman has
written a useful, abbreviated version, published by Management
Pocketbooks, 2001.

● *Zapp! The Lightning of Empowerment*, by William C. Byham
  with Jeff Cox. Development Dimensions International, 1988.
This is presented as an easy-to-read and amusing fable, which,
despite its light-hearted style, nevertheless is a realistic and
practical guide to engaging people and building trust.

● *Mars and Venus in the Workplace*, by John Gray.
  HarperCollins, 2002.
This book provides valuable insights into the secret workings
of Martians and Venusians at work, written as a practical
guide with insights and tips; it is immensely readable and
illuminating.

● *Sex and Business*, by Shere Hite. FT/Prentice Hall, 1999.
Some interesting research with easy-to-read facts and figures.

● *Why Men Don't Listen and Women Can't Read Maps*, by Allan
  and Barbara Pease. Orion, 1999.
Amusing anecdotes and psychological research make this
a fascinating read on men and women in all contexts. The
principles can be extracted easily to apply to the corporate
jungle specifically.

● Biographies and corporate stories are a great source of what's
worked well and what hasn't. For example: *The Rise and Fall of
Marks and Spencer and How it Rose Again*, by Judi Bevan. Profile
Books, 2001, updated in 2007.

Courses

Sales training, for non-sales people too, is something I recommend to enhance skills of influence and persuasion. Take a look at TACK International as just one example (www.tack. co.uk).

Quotes

- 'Neither birth nor sex forms a limit to genius.' Charlotte Bronte

- 'We are what we repeatedly do. Excellence, then, is not an act, but a habit.' Aristotle

- 'I know of no more encouraging fact than the unquestionable ability of man to elevate his life by conscious endeavour.' Henry David Thoreau

- 'If I have the belief that I can do it, I shall surely acquire the capacity to do it, even if I may not have it at the beginning.' Gandhi

- 'What do you need to be the best? Concentration. Discipline. A dream.' Florence Griffith Joyner, Olympic gold medallist

- 'Always bear in mind that your own resolution to succeed is more important than any other one thing.' Abraham Lincoln

- 'Knowing is not enough: we must apply. Willing is not enough: we must do.' Goethe

- 'The less you talk, the more you're listened to.' Abigail van Buren

- 'Do or not do: there is no try.' Yoda, *Star Wars*

- 'Being nice in the office is like being nice on the roads – everyone likes you, but you don't actually get anywhere.' Guy Browning

- 'Excellence is to do a common thing in an uncommon way.' Booker T. Washington

- 'A woman is like a teabag: you never know how strong she is until she gets in hot water.' Eleanor Roosevelt

- 'I hate women because they always know where things are.' James Thurber

- 'Male and female represent the two sides of the great radical dualism ... There is no wholly masculine man, no purely feminine woman.' Margaret Fuller

- 'Women who seek to be equal with men lack ambition.' Timothy Leary

- 'What's the difference between an ordinary woman and an extraordinary woman? The belief that she's ordinary.' Jody Williams, 1997 Nobel Peace Prize Winner

Turn Up The Volume

Books

- *Brand Sense*, by Martin Lindstrom. Kogan Page, 2005.
This is an engaging and lateral approach to branding: the concept of branding across senses makes sense for people, too.

- *Building Strong Brands*, by David Aaker, Simon & Schuster, 2002.
A classic introduction to the subject of branding; it's thorough and comprehensive.

- *Differentiate or Die*, by Jack Trout. John Wiley & Sons, 2000.
Positioning: The Battle for Your Mind, by Jack Trout. McGraw Hill, 1981.
These two titles make fascinating reading and are outstanding as introductions to the fascinating world of marketing and brand positioning.

- *Lovemarks: The Future Beyond Brands*, by Kevin Roberts. Powerhouse Cultural Entertainment Books, 2004.

Gets the reader thinking about how brands can become irresistible rather than respected by adding the 'love' ingredient.

● *NLP Workbook*, by Joseph O'Connor. HarperCollins, 2001. The sections on communication and language are particularly useful in this context.

● *Branding Yourself*, by Mary Spillane. Pan Books, 2000. A basic guide, particularly useful for 'packaging'.

● *Always in Style*, by Doris Pooser. Piatkus, 1987.
Successful Style: A Man's Guide to a Complete Professional Image, by Doris Pooser. Crisp Publications Inc, 1990.
There are masses of image books around but Doris Pooser's are among the best. She covers everything you need to know about dressing with your lines, colours and scale in mind.

● *Eats, Shoots and Leaves*, by Lynne Truss. Profile Books, 2003. Advocating a zero tolerance approach to punctuation, this is a fabulous read and is a must for all of us who are unwittingly cruel to punctuation and strive to do better.

Coaches

In the context of Turn Up The Volume, you may choose to select coaches who specialise in image, voice and presentation techniques to make sure you get the look and sound of your brand congruent and right for you. The best way to find the right person is to get a word-of-mouth recommendation, meet a few coaches and check out the levels of rapport between you.

For image coaches, check out The Federation of Image Consultants (www.tfic.org.uk).

Courses

Acting classes are fun and can hugely help your confidence levels. Specifically, they can teach voice projection, stage presence, improvisation – how to think on your feet. A good place to start looking is your local institute for adult education.

While looking there you'll also find Pilates, Alexander technique and martial arts classes, all of which will be great for posture and developing your grounded physiology. Alternatively, get recommendations from bodies like:

The Pilates Foundation (www.pilatesfoundation.com) or Body Control Pilates (www.bodycontrol.co.uk)

The Society of Teachers of the Alexander Technique (www.stat.org.uk)

Quotes

- 'It is the chiefest point of happiness that a man is willing to be what he is.' Erasmus
- 'In order to be irreplaceable, one must always be different.' Coco Chanel
- 'Be yourself. Be unique and therefore be successful.' Eleanor Roosevelt
- 'Don't compromise yourself; you're all you've got.' Janis Joplin
- 'This above all: to thine own self be true,
  And it must follow, as the night the day,
  Thou canst not then be false to any man.' Shakespeare's *Hamlet*
- 'I am no longer what I was. I will remain what I have become.' Coco Chanel
- 'Life isn't about finding yourself. Life is about creating yourself.' George Bernard Shaw
- 'Clothes make the man. Naked people have little or no influence on society.' Mark Twain
- 'There are no ugly women, only lazy ones'. Helena Rubinstein

- 'People seldom notice old clothes if you wear a big smile.' Lee Mildon
- 'What a strange power there is in clothing.' Isaac Bashevis Singer
- 'Language is very difficult to put into words.' Voltaire
- 'We should have a great fewer disputes in the world if words were taken for what they are, the signs of our ideas only, and not for things themselves.' John Locke

Don't Just Sit There

Books

- *Network Your Way to Success*, by John Timperley. Piatkus, 2002.
  Networking for Everyone, by L. Michelle Tullier. JIST Works, 1998.

These two guides provide comprehensive advice, tools, tips and techniques and just about everything you can think of that relates to networking.

- *The Tipping Point*, by Malcolm Gladwell. Little, Brown, 2000.

Many of Gladwell's concepts are relevant to networking. For example, connectors (sociable personalities who bring people together); mavens (who like to pass along knowledge); and salesmen (adept at persuading).

- *How to Have a Beautiful Mind*, by Edward de Bono. Vermilion, 2004.

Most of the book deals with holding interesting conversations and much of the advice is common sense. The book includes topics such as 'How to be interesting' and 'How to rescue a boring conversation', with generic advice to develop your own store of conversation, anecdotes, jokes.

- *Leaving Microsoft to Change the World*, by John Wood. Collins, 2006.

Wood left his lucrative career with Microsoft and founded Room to Read, a charity providing schools and libraries in deprived parts of the world. Although this inspiring book could equally sit in the Inner Game, with Wood's frog goals and strong values, I've included it here because Room to Read is built on powerful connecting and his funding model is based firmly on local networks. An inspiring read.

Networking organisations

A Google search for business networking organisations will bring up around 4 million results. There are plenty of places to go and each will appeal to different people. Again, personal recommendations and reputation will be the best way to select what's right for you. I just want to mention a couple:

The London Business Forum offers a programme of quality speakers and each meeting is a stimulating learning opportunity in itself, helping you to keep your knowledge current. Having a theme and a focus means that it's relatively easy to get talking to people (www.londonbusinessforum.com).

There is a rising number of internet networking sites. I'm not a great user of these, but people tell me they are great and they may be good for you. In particular, take a look at LinkedIn (www.linkedin.com) and Ecademy (www.ecademy.com).

If you're self-employed, check out BNI, a successful networking group specifically tailored to your market. There are chapters all over the country (www.bni-europe.com).

Quotes

- 'More business decisions occur over lunch and dinner than at any other time, yet no MBA courses are given on the subject.' Peter Drucker
- 'Help others get ahead. You will always stand taller with someone else on your shoulders.' Bob Moawad

- 'I discovered a long time ago that if I helped people get what they wanted, I would always get what I wanted and I would never have to worry.' Anthony Robbins

- 'Do unto others as you would wish them do unto you.' The Ethic of Reciprocity

- 'This I believe: that the free, exploring mind of the individual human is the most valuable thing in the world.' John Steinbeck

- 'Years wrinkle the skin, but to give up enthusiasm wrinkles the soul.' Douglas MacArthur

- 'People, even more than things, have to be restored, renewed, revived, reclaimed and redeemed; never throw out anyone.' Audrey Hepburn

- 'Nature has given to man one tongue, but two ears that we may hear from others twice as much as we speak.' Epictetus, Greek philosopher

- 'Fools talk; cowards are silent; wise men listen.' Carlos Ruiz Zafon, *The Shadow of the Wind*

- 'All publicity is good. Except an obituary notice.' Brendan Behan

- 'Being powerful is like being a lady. If you have to tell people you are, you aren't.' Margaret Thatcher

- 'Many times a day, I realise how much my outer and inner life is built upon the labours of people ... and how earnestly I must exert myself in order to give in return as much as I have received.' Albert Einstein

The checklists

Preparation checklist from The Inner Game

Purpose

- What is the purpose of it?

- What is the outcome you want?

- How do you want people to feel afterwards?

Focus

- What are the issues?

- What do you need to know?

- What do you need to cover?

Target

- Who is your audience? What do you know about them?

- What do they know? What don't they know? What do they want to hear?

- What might they be feeling?

- What are their possible responses? What killer questions might they ask? How will you answer?

Practical stuff

- How much time do you have?

- What do you need to take?

- Where will it take place?

- Where will you sit? Will you stand?

- How will you convey your message? Do you need any visual cues or handouts?

- What will you wear?

Ending

- How will you close?

- What are the next steps?

The SMART+ checklist for creating achievable outcomes

1 Define your outcome in the positive

Ask yourself, 'What do I want?' rather than 'What don't I want?' For example: 'I want to be on the mergers and acquisitions project team', rather than 'I don't want to be left behind'. By the way, losing weight and giving up smoking are negative outcomes and often difficult to achieve; try out instead the goal of becoming healthy.

2 Specific

Know exactly what it is. 'I want a holiday' is too vague. What are the specifics? I want to go away at Christmas, somewhere that will be hot, a twelve-hour maximum flight, somewhere I can speak English, where I won't have jet lag and which won't cost me more than £2,000. You'll probably find yourself setting off for South Africa.

3 Measurable

Define how you will know that you're on track, that you're succeeding. What will the measures be? Feedback or a tangible result like a pay increase, an increase in revenue, a purchase made, a project plan completed on budget and in time? How will you differentiate between acceptable and outstanding performance? What does outstanding look like?

4 Achievable

Do you have the resources you will need and will you have access to them? Resources include things, time, people, money and your own personal skills. Build confidence and belief. Ask yourself: Why will I be good at this? What have I done before that is similar? Who will help me? What self-talk will help me? What beliefs and states will be most useful? What time and effort will this goal need? What will I need to give up and am I prepared to do it? Who else might be affected by my going for this? What impact will it have on them? Am I and are they comfortable that the impact is acceptable? What is good about the status quo? What do I want to keep?

5 Realistic

Is this within your control? Is it too stretching? Can it be done? What are the contingency plans if something goes wrong? How will I keep myself on track? What milestones do I need?

6 Timed

When will you do this? When do you want it? Deadlines provide huge impetus. The football game demands that all is accomplished within a set timeframe and that focuses and drives the players.

The success profile from Be Bloody Good

Knowledge	**Experience**
Strengths	Strengths
What I want to enhance	What I want to enhance
What I plan to do, specifically	What I plan to do, specifically

Competencies	**Personal traits**
Strengths	Strengths
What I want to enhance	What I want to enhance/ check
What I plan to do, specifically	What I plan to do, specifically

Glossary

Brighton rock	A consistent brand message
Bumblebee	Just getting on with it; why, rather than why not
Cashmere socks	A trance-like state for creative thinking
Connector	Someone who acts as a hub for connecting people together
Crazy paving	Career planning by serendipity; slab by slab
EQ or EI	Emotional Intelligence Quotient
Frog thinking	Thinking big (outside the well)
In charge	Taking responsibility for yourself: getting results instead of giving reasons or excuses
IQ	Intelligence Quotient
Jane	Man or woman with orientation to 'female style'
Neuro-Linguistic Programming (NLP)	Models how we think, use language and act to provide tools for achieving our goals
Poor me	Not taking responsibility and waiting for your fairy godmother
Relator	Someone who enjoys meaningful relationships and wants to understand others' feelings

Roast beef	The need to update beliefs and decisions
Stuffed mushrooms	Knowing what's not important so you can focus on what is
Tarzan	Man or woman with orientation to 'male' style
Tough empathy	Telling people what they need to know not what they want to know.
Transformational style	Motivational and supportive (Jane)
Transactional style	'Command and control' (Tarzan)
Woo	A strength describing someone who enjoys meeting new people and initiating conversations

Acknowledgements

In the course of my work and while researching for the book, I've read so much: from entry permit, magazines, books and the internet. I've heard so much: from random conversations, talks, lectures, radio and TV. When it came to it, I sat down and wrote the book from what was in my head. Although I believe I've attributed and acknowledged material whenever it was due, it's possible that something may have slipped my memory. If I have failed to acknowledge appropriately, I apologise: do let me know and I'll rectify my omission on my website and in future editions.

Here's my Oscar list of people to thank:

Pat Lomax: thank you so much for believing in my manuscript and seeing its potential from the very beginning. Your red pen was an excruciating experience but I now admit that it served me well.

Daniel Crewe: a Bloody Good editor – I'm in awe of your skill with words, but it's for your respect and sensitivity that I thank you (and Penny Williams for the final gloss).

The role models: your stories inspired and moved me. I battled to include everything you told me but was overruled time and time again, by that same nice editor who can be surprisingly tough when it comes down to it.

Profile Books: huge thanks for recognising Tarzan and Jane and for welcoming me into your midst. And special thanks to Paul Forty and Ben Usher.

Abigail Sharan: thanks for introducing me to the many lovely people at Microsoft that I met through *Tarzan and Jane*: Helen, Susanne, Neil, Maureen, Trisha. You'll have spotted, too, that I used your invaluable overview of product branding.

Rick and Jacquelyn Lane: for getting me started, and for introducing me to 'The Idiot's Guide to Getting Published'.

Ian and Gary: without your firm nagging I'd never have stayed in my office long enough to write anything.

Rod Stewart: I played his mellow American smooth albums over and over and over. And over. What a great sound to write to.

Jeff Grout: you old hippy. Your abundant and generous networking led me to Diana Boulter, Roz Savage and Pat Lomax, who became my agent.

The White Company: for my well-worn cream, pink and beige cashmere socks.

Irene Nathan: for your cutting-edge advice on clothes and image. Must book another session for myself!

My practitioner buddies: midwives at the birth of the book.

Laura Lewin: for the 'object' exercise – I still love it!

Philip Whiteley: for quality coaching and letting me use your great quote to promote the book.

Women In Finance Networking Group: for your input to Tarzan and Jane differences.

All my fabulous friends: for your sheer fabulousness, friendship and constant encouragement.

My warm, lovely, large and extended family: all of you – near and far, always there, always supportive, always fun – you know how much you mean to me.

Orly: your excitement for the project was gorgeously infectious from the outset and I'm still using that lovely purple 'Ah ha' book for all my quotes.

Jonathan: you got me started with all your clever advice about framework and structure. Notice how well I listened.

The Lor and the Ha: with love and thanks for absolutely everything – from the right genes to a lemonade mindset, from endless encouragement to skilled proofreading. You're my role models.

Daniel, Eliot, Adam and now Tzvi: the adored boys in my life, for being utterly gorgeous people, for keeping me real, for being there.

Aaron: my best mate, for breakfasts in bed, endless cups of tea, for doing all the shopping, for all the yummy cooking, for managing the house, for litmus test reading, for good-naturedly enduring Rod Stewart, for answering the phone, for massages and laughter, for bucket loads of love and for believing in me.

References

Theme 1 The Inner Game

The title of this section was inspired by W. Timothy Galwey's *Inner Game of Tennis*, Random House, 1997 (first published 1974).

1 Turknett Leadership Group, Atlanta, GA, USA.
2 *ITS Report*, 8 December 2004, Queen's University, Belfast (on behalf of ITS, a training consultancy, www.itsconsult.com).
3 Joseph O'Connor, *NLP Workbook*, HarperCollins, 2001.
4 Stephen Covey, *The 7 Habits of Highly Effective People*, Free Press, 1989.
5 Shirley Conran, *Superwoman*, Sidgwick & Jackson, 1975.
6 Barbara Oaff, "Job-sharing", *Guardian Unlimited* (jobsadvice. guardian.co.uk/lifeandwork/story/0,,1181102,00.html).
7 Business Link guide developed by the Department of Trade and Industry in 2006.
8 Claude Steiner, *Scripts People Live*, Grove Press, 1974.
9 Adapted from Landmark Education, The Landmark Forum: Advanced Course (www.landmarkforum.com).
10 Stephen Covey, op. cit.
11 Pat Heim and Susan Golant, *Hardball for Women*, Plume, 1992.

Theme 2 Be Bloody Good

1 Marcus Buckingham and Donald O. Clifton, *Now, Discover Your Strengths*, Simon & Schuster, 2002.

2 Adapted from *Leadership 2010: The Conference Board Report*, 2002, in conjunction with Development Dimensions International.

3 Adapted from Mary Spillane, *Branding Yourself*, Pan, 2000.

4 Adapted with permission from Development Dimensions International (DDI).

5 Stephen Covey, op. cit.

6 Daniel Goleman, *Emotional Intelligence: Why It Can Matter More Than IQ*, Bantam, reprinted 1997.

7 Included in DDI's Job Satisfaction Factors.

8 Adapted from the Boston EI Questionnaire and DDI's key principles self-evaluation.

9 'What they need is a damn good listening to: buyers' views of salespeople', *Changing Perceptions*, TACK International (www.tack.co.uk).

10 Juan Villalonga in Shere Hite, *Sex and Business*, FT/Prentice Hall, 1999.

11 John Gray, *Mars and Venus in the Workplace*, HarperCollins, 2002.

12 Pat Heim, op. cit.

13 Ibid.

14 John Gray, op. cit.

15 Deborah Tannen, *You Just Don't Understand*, Virago Press, 1991.

16 Punch Ltd 2003.

Theme 3 Turn Up The Volume

1 Martin Lindstrom, *Brand Sense*, Kogan Page, 2005.

2 Kevin Roberts, *Lovemarks: The Future Beyond Brands*, Powerhouse Cultural Entertainment Books, 2004.

3 David A. Aaker, *Building Strong Brands*, Simon & Schuster, 2002.

4 Albert Mehrabian, *Silent Messages*, Wadsworth, 1971.

5 John Timperley, *Network Your Way to Success*, Piatkus, 2002.

6 *USA Today*, 24 September 2003, reporting on the luxury goods market. A DTI fashion report reported revenues of £600 million in the UK even in 1998.

Theme 4 Don't Just Sit There

1 Marcus Buckingham and Donald O. Clifton, op. cit.
2 Malcolm Gladwell, *The Tipping Point*, Little, Brown, 2000.
3 Cheryl Travers and Carole Pemberton, 'Understanding Networking as a Culturally Differentiated Career Skill', in Marilyn J. Davidson and Ronald J. Burke (eds), *Women in Management*, Vol. II, Ashgate, 2004.
4 Cited in Marilyn J. Davidson and Ronald J. Burke, op. cit.
5 Ibid.
6 Ibid.
7 Ibid.
8 Ibid.
9 Ibid.
10 John Timperley, op. cit.
11 Daniel Goleman, *Social Intelligence*, Bantam, 2006; to be published by Random House, 2007.

5 The Leader's Part

1 Marilyn J. Davidson and Ronald J. Burke, op. cit.
2 Marilyn J. Davidson and Ronald J. Burke, op. cit.; the Equal Opportunities Commission (EOC), *Sex and Power: Who Runs Britain in 2007?*
3 'Rambos in Pinstripes: why so many CEOs are lousy leaders', L. Grant, *Fortune*, Vol. 133, Issue 12, 1999.
4 Marilyn J. Davidson and Ronald J. Burke, op. cit.

6 Making It Stick

1 Mike Ditka and Tom Laundry, *The World of Pro Football*, Book Sales, 1987.
2 Chartered Institute of Personnel and Development (CIPD), *Coaching at Work*, 2006.